HEROES OF THE CROSS

Twentieth Century Men of Faith
of The Methodist Church in Estonia

Compiled by Toomas Pajusoo

Tallinn 2007

Originally published in Estonian under the title *Eesti ristikangelasi.
Peatükke Eesti Metodisti Kiriku XX sajandi usukangelastest.*
Compiled by Toomas Pajusoo. Tallinn 2006
© Toomas Pajusoo, 2006
Published with the support of The United Methodist Publishing House.

*Heroes of The Cross. Twentieth Century Men of Faith
of The Methodist Church in Estonia*
Translated by Kai-Ines Nelson
Edited by Mark P. Nelson
Proofreading by Norma Bates
Cover design by Piibe Piirma
Publishing adviser Tarmo Lilleoja

© Eesti Metodisti Kirik, 2007

This book has been published with the support of the Council of Estonian
Churches as well as Alison & Robert F. Hogan, Jr., from Houston, Texas

ISBN 978-1-7345199-9-0
Published in English by WesleyMen, Inc., 2022

*On the front cover, photos from top left, moving clockwise: Martin Prikask,
Aleksander Kuum, Jaan Jaagupsoo with Irene and Anne, Peeter Häng (two
photos), Martin Prikask, Vassili Prii (center).*

*On the back cover, photos from top left, moving clockwise: Liisi and Martin
Prikask, Hugo Oengo, Jaan Jaagupsoo, Vassili Prii, Agathe and Aleksander
Kuum, Aleksander Kuum, Hugo Oengo.*

"Like the author of the Letter to the Hebrews who, having described the victorious life of many an Old Testament man of faith, suddenly asked himself the following question: 'And what more shall I say?. . . ' I lack the time (and space) to tell you about Prikask, the church leader who during the reign of Red Terror was privileged to suffer martyrdom along with pastors Vassili Prii, Peeter Häng, and Jaan Jaagupsoo. It would be hard to keep silent about the honored church leaders such as Aleksander Kuum, who according to the plan of the Soviet occupying powers should have ended his days in Siberia, or Hugo Oengo who - upon having been made to choose by the very same political authorities - gave up a prestigious career as a scientist for the sake of the Gospel of Christ. There is so much to be told about these contemporary heroes of faith, men and women, whose names have been kept in the dark from the wider public, but not from God: 'A scroll of remembrance was written in his presence concerning those who feared the Lord and honored his name' (Malachi 3:16). Therefore – nothing has been forgotten in the highest level of the universe. "In dishonor sowed, in glory raised again!' (1 Corinthians 15:43, adapted)."

Olav Pärnamets Superintendent emeritus of The UMC in Estonia
UMC in Estonia's Magazine *Koduteel* 7/1997, p. 7.

TABLE OF CONTENTS

FOREWORD

". . . and honor people like him" (Philippians 2:29)

In 2007, The United Methodist Church (UMC) in Estonia celebrated her 100th jubilee. The beginnings of Methodism in Estonia can be traced back to 1907, a time when Estonia was still but a province of Imperial Russia. At that time, Bishop William Burt appointed a young and energetic American, Dr. George Albert Simons (1874–1952), as superintendent to the Russia Mission to pioneer the Methodist work in St. Petersburg, then capital city of Russia. In the Methodist congregation in St. Petersburg the work grew by leaps and bounds. It was there that Vassili Täht, a young Estonian man working for the British and Foreign Bible Society, heard of Methodists for the very first time.

The exact date and place that can be pinpointed as the birth of Methodism in Estonia is June 9, 1907, in Arensburg (modern-day Kuressaare), the main city on the island of Saaremaa, situated just off the western coast of the mainland. Upon his return to his native country, it was there that Vassili Täht together with his friend Karl Kuum, a Moravian lay preacher, started proclaiming the gospel. At first the worship services were held in private homes; however, in 1910, the first Methodist congregation was founded in Kuressaare, in the residence of a local church member. Vassili Täht was appointed as the pastor to the newly founded church, a position soon filled by Martin Prikask, who later became the superintendent. The very first Methodist church building in Estonia, a modest wooden structure, was consecrated in 1912 and is still in use today.

After more than 100 years of Methodism in Estonia, we invite you on a brief journey through the stories of these remarkable men whom God has used as tools of his grace. It is our wish that the blessing they have brought to the Estonian people would be shared beyond our borders and become a blessing for the body of Christ worldwide.

This book contains biographies of three superintendents of the Episcopal and later United Methodist Church in Estonia: **Martin Prikask**, **Hugo Oengo**, and **Aleksander Kuum**. As the presiding Methodist bishop for Estonia has always lived in another country (and after World War II on the opposite side of the Iron Curtain), these are the men who had responsibility for the daily leadership of Methodism in Estonia. They are the heroes who brought us from our beginnings through the joyous years in which Estonia established a successful independent and democratic state. They faithfully led us through the tragedy of seeing our freedom crushed under the heels of the Red Army, through Stalinist terror, and the worst of Soviet persecution. Through their leadership, Estonia would become the only place inside the Soviet Union where Methodism visibly survived as an active, public, and connected testimony to the gospel of Jesus Christ.[1] In accomplishing this remarkable feat, these men have become more than simply the heroes of Estonian Methodism,

---

[1] It should be noted that there were two underground Methodist groups meeting in western Ukraine (Ushgorod and Kaminica) throughout the Soviet period. They bravely continued beneath the public radar, despite being practically unconnected and without episcopal leadership. In the 1960's Estonian Methodists became aware of these groups; and Estonian leaders, including then-superintendent, Olav Pärnamets, made difficult journeys to meet with and encourage them. Today, these courageous Methodists are thriving. We wish God's blessings upon these our brothers and sisters and wait for the day when they will tell the world their stories.

they have become heroes for Christians of all denominations and in all countries.

Martin Prikask (1877–1942) was the very first Estonian superintendent and martyr of the Estonian Methodist Church[2], who died in Siberia. He is rightfully considered one of the outstanding heroes of faith of our church and is widely respected among the wider Estonian Christian circle. It is perhaps fitting that in 2007, as The UMC in Estonia celebrated its 100th anniversary, we will also remembered Reverend Prikask's 130th birthday and the 65th anniversary of his death.

In recording the biography of Martin Prikask, I have tapped into various source materials. The bulk of the information I have received from the Methodist magazine *Kristlik Kaitsja (Christian Advocate)*. In November 1977, as a part of celebrations dedicated to commemorate Martin Prikask's 100th birthday, Superintendent Hugo Oengo wrote an article called "Fragments of Biography," which was sent out as a circular letter to all the Methodist congregations in Estonia. Oengo's article is largely based upon the articles in the Methodist gazette as well as Elmar Palumäe's article on Martin Prikask written in 1974, entitled "Words of Life from Many Lips," which was hand typed and distributed at the time, unfortunately not without some discrepancies.

All the above-mentioned sources were carefully examined, compiled, and published by the author of this book in the Methodist magazine *Koduteel* in 2002. In compiling this book, additional records and sources were used as well as some rare

---

[2] As will be explained later in the book, the original name of the church was the "Methodist Episcopal Church in Estonia." However in 1940 the name was officially changed to "Estonian Methodist Church" (Eesti Metodisti Kirik). Following the formation of The United Methodist Church in 1968, the official English name would become "The United Methodist Church in Estonia." Throughout this book we attempt to use the name that was official at the time of the events described. (Translator's note)

photos from the earlier period of The Methodist Church in Estonia.

I have included a separate chapter of memoirs about Martin Prikask that were handwritten by the former pastor of the Kuressaare UMC Congregation, Johannes Truu. These were handed to me by the late deacon of the Tallinn UMC Congregation, Johannes-Leopold Klementi.

Hugo Oengo (1907–1978), whose given names were Hugo Arnold Öngo-Oengo, is the third giant of faith in the history of The UMC in Estonia. And so it is fitting that, in 2007, The UMC in Estonia celebrated her 100th jubilee as well as the 100th anniversary of Hugo Oengo's birth.

Hugo Oengo joined The Methodist Church in 1929. In the summer of 1939 he was ordained as deacon and in 1953 as an elder. From 1935 to 1936 he served as a pastor in Tartu Second Methodist Church. From 1939 to 1941 and again from 1944 until his death, he served in Tallinn Methodist Church. Between those two terms as a pastor in Tallinn were years spent in the Soviet Union during World War II, where he served as a professor in the Ural Industrial Institute in the city of Sverdlovsk. Between 1974 and 1978 Hugo Oengo served as superintendent of The United Methodist Church in Estonia. From 1976 until his death, he belonged to the World Methodist Executive Committee.

Hugo Oengo joined his Maker on December 10, 1978, and his earthly remains are awaiting resurrection in Tallinn's Rahumäe Cemetery. Hugo Oengo was a charismatic personality who possessed an exceptional gift of teaching that was brilliantly employed both at the Tallinn Technical University and in his congregation. Thanks to his faithful prayers many people came to know the Lord and experience healing through Christ. For the sake of the Lord, Oengo gave up promotions in his career and glorious titles of recognition from the government. Regardless, his scientific work was held in high esteem and his expert professional opinion was valued among his colleagues. I came to the Lord having heard Brother Oengo preach the gospel, for which privilege I am eternally grateful.

In this book I have mainly used Hugo Oengo's personal hand-typed autobiographical notes, to which I have added available secondary sources.

Aleksander Kuum (1899–1989) himself wrote a brief autobiographical summary at the age of 59, called "Pages from the Book of My Life," on which I have elaborated in the form of subheadings and extra photo material from the church's archive as well as private collections. Unfortunately, this autobiography covers merely two-thirds of Aleksander Kuum's adventurous life and ends on March 17, 1959. Also it does not cover his Siberian experience in sufficient detail. This last point can be explained by the fact that he was still living under the same totalitarian Soviet regime that had imprisoned him and continued to keep a repressive watch on all that was said and done. To be more specific, it was not safe for him to write clearly about the suffering he endured.

Aleksander Kuum was superintendent of The Estonian Methodist Church between 1962 and 1975 and again from 1978 to 1979. He used to say, *I have served the Methodist Churches in* Tapa, Tartu, *and* Tallinn. *All of these place names start with the letter "T" and now I await with excitement going to my last place of service—"Taevas"* (heaven, in Estonian). He arrived at his heavenly place of dwelling on February 12, 1989. He is buried at Tallinn's Rahumäe Cemetery. We remember Aleksander Kuum as a minister who truly was a shepherd and whose dedicated work has borne rich fruit.

In addition to the superintendents mentioned above, I am also covering recollections concerning three Methodist pastors and great men of faith. These are **Jaan Jaagupsoo** (1898–1941), **Peeter Häng** (1900–1942), and **Vassili Prii** (1909–1942). Jaan Jaagupsoo, as our first martyr, was executed by the special operations unit of the Soviet secret police. Peeter Häng and Vassili Prii died in prison camps in Siberia. The apostle Paul calls upon us to respect men like these who have perished for the sake of Christ's work and did not spare themselves.

"Am I a soldier of the cross?" asks Isaac Watts in his well-known hymn. These men whom you read about in this book were true soldiers of the cross, whom God was able to use for the sake of pouring out his blessings upon many. It is my desire, that the dedicated life and example of the Estonian Methodist heroes of the cross would inspire every reader to serve the Lord faithfully and honor his holy name in their land, wherever that may be.

Toomas Pajusoo, September 9, 2006, Tallinn

TRANSLATOR'S COMMENTS TO THE ENGLISH EDITION

The English edition of this book has been revised and edited to provide background information for the benefit of the English-speaking reader. This includes paragraphs concerning Estonia's history as well as explanatory glosses and footnotes.

The major addition for the English version is a section written by Superintendent Emeritus of The UMC in Estonia, Olav Pärnamets, giving a personal account of the story of Aleksander Kuum.

In regards to the English edition, it should be noted that all dates in this book are given according to the Gregorian calendar commonly used today. The Russian Empire, and therefore also Estonia prior to 1918, used the Julian calendar. Events dated prior to 1900 would therefore, in the original sources be dated as occurring 12 days earlier, and events between 1900 and 1918 would be dated as occurring 13 days earlier due to the discrepancy in the calendar systems. For the sake of simplicity and clarity it was decided to keep all dates in the modern Gregorian system.

The original Estonian version of this book, published in 2006, includes complete referencing to allow the reader to go back to the original sources. However, as the vast majority of these sources are available only in the Estonian language, it is assumed that the reader of the English edition does not require the clutter of referencing. A bibliography of sources is included at the end of this book; nonetheless, those requiring more precise referencing are kindly asked to consult the Estonian original.

Kai Nelson, March 27, 2007, Tallinn

Superintendent and Martyr

Martin Prikask

(November 19, 1877 – September 9, 1942)

I *have fought the good fight, I have finished the race, I have kept the faith. Now there is in store for me the crown of righteousness, which the Lord, the righteous Judge, will award to me on that day – and not only to me, but also to all who have longed for his appearing.*
2 Timothy 4:7–8

Martin Prikask, a photograph from the archives of Saaremaa Museum.

THE EARLY YEARS

History makes curious twists and turns. In Estonia, the administrative borders of the local parishes and townships have shifted from time to time, crossing over to one or the other neighboring county. For this reason it is not an easy task to pinpoint the exact birthplace of the very first superintendent and martyr of Estonian Methodism. To complicate the matter further, Estonia at the time of Martin Prikask's birth had been a part of the Russian Empire since being conquered by Peter the Great one and a half centuries earlier. The southern Viljandimaa district in which the Prikask family lived had been incorporated into a larger province called Livonia, which also included much of what is now the country of Latvia.

In searching for the birthplace of Martin Prikask, three differing sources are available that can be compared with the registry of parishes listed between 1866 and 1917, in the electronic data base of the Estonian Historical Archives. What are these sources?

First of all, I have used the personal autobiographical notes of Martin Prikask himself. In a letter to Ms. Salme Klaos, a postgraduate student at the University of Tartu, he states that his place of birth is the parish of Halliste in the district of Uue-Kariste, but fails to specify the exact location. Maybe he did not consider the exact location of great importance or he was content to stress his regional Mulgi pride[3]. He certainly remembers the Uue-Kariste district with great warmth, making it likely that this was his childhood home.

Second, the Methodist magazine, *Kristlik Kaitsja (Christian Advocate)*, gives a scanty summary, stating that Prikask was born in Viljandimaa district, in the parish of Halliste.

Third, the entry in the church records of the Halliste congregation of the Estonian Evangelical Lutheran Church in 1877, shows that his birth was registered in the county of Kaarli, which, under the German name of Karlsberg, was connected to the large Õisu estate, and belonged until 1877 to the Viljandimaa administrative district before being transferred to the neighboring Pärnu district. This would confirm the information concerning his place of birth given in the article of *Kristlik Kaitsja*.

According to the church records, the parents named their son, born at 3 P.M. on November 19, 1877, Märt Prikask. As this

---

[3] "Mulgimaa" is the name popularly given to the region in southern part of Viljandimaa. It is known as an area of rich farmland and distinct cultural identity. *(Translator's note)*

is the only record of him being called Märt, it is possible that it is a simple mistake on the part of the individual who entered it into the church records. Perhaps the fact that all church records at this time were in German could have contributed to the confusion. The boy was christened on December 3, 1877, in the Lutheran Church in Halliste.

Martin's father was named Frits and mother Leena (maiden name Laredei). In addition to Martin their children also included older children: a son Peeter (b. 1873)[4] and a daughter Ann (b. 1885, married name Undriste). The original form of their last name was Prikask, although at times the spelling was standardized as Priikask.

The time of Martin's childhood coincided with the flourishing of the Mulgimaa region during the last half of the 19th century and the early decades of the 20th century, when the Mulgi peasants in southern Viljandimaa were among the first to purchase their own farmland after being freed from slavery.[5] This allows us to speculate that he had a secure and carefree childhood. According to the popular song lyrics: *"In Mulgimaa the life is good, with beautiful nature and deep forests surrounding you, the fields are bearing good crops and farms are well-to-do."* Growing up in a peasant family, he was raised amidst nature's bounty: the beauty of the delicate wildflowers, the pleasant chorus of songbirds. This peaceful upbringing no doubt aided

[4] Martin's brother Peeter owned the Killamäe farm in Penuja parish. He acted as the head of the local rural municipal government, the head of Penuja Educational Society (later as honorary member), the head of Penuja Mutual Insurance Society, founding member and board member of the Penuja Dairy Society, member as well as the parish clerk of the Halliste Lutheran church. During the Soviet occupation he was deported to Siberia, namely to Krasnoyarsk Krai administrative region. After being released and allowed to return to Estonia, he died in 1957 in Penuja and is buried in the Halliste church yard.

[5] Estonia was invaded and occupied by German knights in the 13th century leading to the Estonian people being eventually reduced to slavery that was finally abolished in 1861. *(Translator's note)*

his emotional perception and development as a sensitive and harmonious individual, tenderhearted, kind, well-meaning, and gifted in music, particularly in singing. Undoubtedly, a major role in his life was played by his parents who raised him to be a God-fearing man.

However, this was also the era known for *Russification*, when Imperial Russian policy attempted to suppress Estonian culture and Estonian language. As a result, Martin's education would begin not in Estonian, but in the Russian language in 1888 in the Kööni Orthodox Church's school located in Õisu parish and then also at the Tuhalaane parish school between 1889 and 1890. In the winter of 1891 he also took Lutheran religious education at the Pahuvere school. In 1891, Martin joined Paistu Lutheran Congregation, where a well-known writer, Jaan Bergmann, served as pastor at the time. It is there where he also was confirmed on November 5, 1895.

The fact that between 1892 and 1895 Martin was able to continue his education at one of the most prestigious private schools in Estonia, the Hugo Treffner High School in the city of Tartu, where many Estonian statesmen as well as members of the intelligentsia had studied, suggests that his parents were financially secure. Through his studies, he became fluent in Russian and German and later also in English, which enabled him to converse freely with the bishop of The Methodist Episcopal Church, Raymond J. Wade, who served as bishop between 1928 and 1946.

His student years in Tartu, influenced by some of his friends and teachers, robbed him of his childlike faith in God. Nevertheless, from time to time he felt a certain "sensation in his heart, as if a voice told him: 'Believe in God!'"

Upon his graduation from the Hugo Treffner High School, Martin Prikask worked as a teacher at Pahuvere School. During 1897 he worked on a farm and between 1898 and 1899 in Tartu as a clerk. While living in Tartu he joined the Peetri congregation of the Estonian Lutheran Church. Then he spent six long years of military service as a musician in the St. Petersburg Russian Imperial Marine Cadet Corps (1900–1906). His army service proved to be very beneficial in refining his musical skills as a songwriter.

When he was released from the army in 1906, Prikask arrived in the city of Arensburg (modern-day Kuressaare), on the Estonian island of Saaremaa. Why he chose to make such an unfavorable move, from wealthy *Mulgimaa* to a poorer part of the country, is not known. It is possible that the reason lies in his marriage to devout Liisi Abi (also spelled Abbi), who was originally from the nearby island of Abruka, where she was born July 5, 1880. According to the Saaremaa newspaper *Meie Maa*, Martin and Liisi were married on May 27, 1906. According to Ida Lõhmus, a member of the Kuressaare Methodist Congregation, Prikask had been sent to the island of Abruka as a schoolmaster and most likely it is there and then that the future couple met. After his marriage, Prikask regained his faith. Martin had a very special relationship with his wife. He treated her with exceptional love and respect, so much so that it was noticed as being more than is normally present between spouses.

As a capable young man with a good head for business, Prikask opened a small shop in the city of Kuressaare and worked as a shopkeeper for two years (1907–1908). Most likely he would have remained a businessman if God had not made other plans for his life.

MARTIN PRIKASK AND THE PREACHING BROTHERS

For Martin Prikask the spiritual breakthrough came in 1907, when two preaching brothers, as they were popularly called at the time, Vassili Täht and Karl Kuum launched a series of evangelistic meetings in Arensburg (Kuressaare) on June 9. This date is now considered the start of The Methodist Church in Estonia.

However, the roots of the Methodist revival in Estonia lead to Imperial Russia. In 1907, Bishop William Burt, residing in Zürich, appointed Dr. George Albert Simons to be the superintendent and treasurer of Russia and Finland. Dr. Simons began work in the Methodist Episcopal Church in St. Petersburg, Russia, part of the Finland and St. Petersburg Mission which had been established in 1892. An Estonian man, Vassili Täht, who was originally from the island of Saaremaa and who at the time worked for the British and Foreign Bible Society as a door-to-door salesman, happened to come to St. Petersburg at the same time.

The first Methodist preacher in Estonia, Vassili Täht from Saaremaa (on the right).

There is an interesting story told about Dr. Simons, which goes as follows. He had been learning Russian and was able to speak a little of the language when one day he went to town without a translator. Having reached a street corner, he saw a man approaching. An inner voice made him stop; the other man also halted. The two men looked at each other and the stranger asked in Russian: "Are you a believer?" The American responded: "Yes!" The stranger was Vassili Täht. When exactly Täht accepted Jesus Christ as his personal Savior is not known; however, while in St. Petersburg he established good contacts with the local Methodists and became a member of the local congregation. Dr. Simons saw a potential in him for expanding the mission work and sent him to Estonia.

Upon his arrival on the island of Saaremaa, Vassili Täht met Karl Kuum, a lay preacher from the Moravian Church, originally from the city of Tapa in Virumaa, in the northeastern region of Estonia. Together these two men put on lively and well-attended evangelistic meetings in private homes, which brought on the spiritual revival in the area. The very first meeting was held in the residence of local merchant Mihkel Trey in Kuressaare. Martin Prikask frequented these meetings and committed his life to the Lord on June 27, 1907, sharing this blessing with his wife, Liisi.

His conversion gave Prikask a whole new objective for his life. Following his salvation, he longed to tell people about the grace of God that he had experienced. His first sermon was preached on August 19, 1907, and from this point on, the motto of his life could be conveyed in the words of John Wesley: *"I look upon all the world as my parish . . . and my bounden duty, to declare unto all that are willing to hear, the glad tidings of salvation"* (Journal entry of June 11, 1739).

THE MINISTRY BEGINS

Martin Prikask played a significant part in the launch and development of The Methodist Episcopal Church in Estonia: he was the first superintendent of Estonian descent (serving from

1921 to 1922; 1928 to 1941); a church planter; an esteemed teacher; and a superb preacher, writer, and publisher, as well as martyr.

Unfortunately there are insufficient documents available that would give a more detailed picture of his activities between 1907 and April of 1920. It is only between May 1920 and July 1940 that we are able to follow the events of day-to-day business of The Methodist Episcopal Church in Estonia. Prior to 1920, some light can be shed from the pages of the Methodist magazine *Kristlik Kaitsja (Christian Advocate)*, which was published by Martin Prikask.

It is known that in 1908 Prikask gave up shopkeeping and dedicated himself completely to preaching the gospel. He worked side-by-side with Mihkel Trey, an acquaintance from his days as a merchant and later his fellow believer, as a small group leader for the new converts.

The first visit by Superintendent Dr. George A. Simons to the island of Saaremaa in 1909 did not yet result in the formal establishing of the Methodist congregation, although it had been nearly two years since Täht and Kuum had started the revival movement. In one of his articles, entitled "The Development and Annual Conferences of The Methodist Church in Estonia," Prikask writes that Holy Communion was first observed in the fall of 1908 in one of the Kuressaare homes. The Kuressaare Methodist Congregation was officially established on August 26, 1910, at 10 P.M., when Superintendent Dr. George A. Simons and Vassili Täht accepted three men and three women as the first members of The Methodist Episcopal Church in Estonia. The ceremony took place at Mrs. Vildenberg's residence in Kohtu Street 2. By the end of the year the congregation had grown by 17 female members, and by 1924 the number of members in the Kuressaare church reached 366 people.

Starting in 1910, Martin Prikask evangelized as an authorized lay preacher mainly in the rural areas, while Vassili Täht remained active in the city. Täht also participated as the first ever Estonian in the Finnish Annual Conference held in Mikkeli, Finland, in 1910, where he was formally appointed as preacher to Kuressaare. Later, Täht would be sent by Superintendent Simons to serve in Russia, where he disappears from the historical sources.

Kuressaare church building in the early days.

Prikask's efforts bore good fruit and the Methodist work grew. On July 25, 1910, Reeküla Methodist Congregation was founded. This congregation remains vital today and is the oldest Methodist congregation in Estonia, being officially founded one month before the "mother congregation" in Kuressaare. Next came the Tõlluste congregation, founded on September 8, 1910. At the time both Reeküla and Tõlluste remained affiliates of the Kuressaare congregation, and they do not appear as separate congregations even in the lists of congregations of The Methodist Episcopal Church of Estonia that were presented to the Minister of Internal Affairs for approval in 1935 and 1940. This was typical of the organization system of The Methodist Church at this time. For example in 1924 there were 13 divisions of Methodist work in Saaremaa, all under the umbrella of the Kuressaare congregation.

God poured out his blessing upon the mission work of Dr. Simons, which grew in the Russian Empire, which at that time included Finland and the three Baltic countries, Estonia, Latvia, and Lithuania. In Vaasa, Finland, in 1911, Finland became a separate annual conference, and the Russia Mission was officially founded. Prikask was present as one of the founding members of the Russia Mission but continued to participate in the activities of the Finnish Annual Conference as well. From the records of the 1911 conference one may find Prikask's name appearing for the first time among the appointees of the Russia Mission to Arensburg (Kuressaare) by Bishop William Burt. It is in Finland that Prikask started his theological studies; and, while participating in six Finnish Annual Conferences between 1911 and 1916, he passed all the necessary exams and completed the five-year theological study course required to become an ordained Methodist clergyman. Martin Prikask worked as the pastor of Kuressaare congregation from his first appointment until 1921, at the same time being active in mission work across the entire island.

In July 1912, the Russia Mission held its second conference in Kovno (present day Kaunas, Lithuania) led by Bishop Dr. John L. Nuelsen and consisting of 12 believers: Dr. George A. Simons, Martin Prikask, Leo P. Heinrich, Vassili Täht, Nikolai P. Oksotsky, Emil Ricken, Paul Ludvig, Alfred Hühn, August Karlson, George E. Durdis, Aarno Tuulihovi, and Karl Kuum. The conference of the Russia Mission in Kovno was held in the very first Methodist church building erected in Imperial Russia, consecrated by Bishop William Burt on January 14, 1911. On July 15, 1912, the first congregation was founded on the Estonian mainland in the city of Tapa and included 10 members. Another landmark in the Methodist revival movement was the opening of Estonia's first Methodist church building in Kuressaare, which was consecrated on October 28, 1912. The construction was financed by Martin Prikask himself. As a former businessman, he was financially able to donate 10,000 rubles for the cause. The church building was formally registered in his name as his private property since there was no other way to arrange it in accordance with the laws of the Russian Empire. After Estonia declared her independence in 1918, under an Estonian government these funds were reimbursed to him by the American Missions Society.

ORDINATION

A wholly different and somewhat complicated matter to establish is Martin Prikask's ordination. One of the sources available, *Kristlik Kaitsja (Christian Advocate)* magazine, states that Prikask was ordained as deacon by Bishop John Louis Nuelsen in 1912 and as elder (pastor by profession) in 1915. A Saaremaa newspaper, *Meie Maa*, states without mentioning the exact date that Prikask was ordained as a pastor by Bishop John L. Nuelsen and Dr. Lemuel H. Murlin, president of the University of Boston. The second source available to us is Prikask's personal letter to Salme Klaos, a postgraduate student at the University of Tartu, which unfortunately serves only to complicate the matter. In his letter Prikask says that he was ordained by Bishop Burt as a deacon in 1913. Due to the very limited source material it is very difficult to verify this statement. There are two options: Prikask made a mistake or his ordination took place at the conference of the Russia Mission since the reports of the Finnish Annual Conferences between 1912 and 1916 do not support this claim.

It should be noted that in those days Methodist clergy had a two-tier ordination process, first as deacon, then elder. A few brothers, including Prikask, were a part of the Russia Mission and participated in the Finnish Annual Conference beginning in 1912. Therefore they took part in two conferences. In the matter of Prikask's ordination, the archives of The Methodist Church in Finland have new light to shed.

In 1913, the Finnish Annual Conference was held in the city of Turku from July 31 to August 8. According to the yearbook of The Methodist Episcopal Church, Prikask was accepted as a probationary member of the annual conference only in 1912. Together with Prikask, a number of probationary members were accepted, namely Alfred Hühn from Riga, Latvia; Paul Ludvig from Kovno (present day Kaunas), Lithuania; Nikolai P. Oksotsky from St. Petersburg, Russia, and Toivo Rajalinna from Kuopio, Finland. According to the list of appointments coming out of the 1913 conference, Prikask is appointed to Arensburg (Kuressaare). There is also a remark in the yearbook concerning his theological studies, where in section 27 it states that Martin Prikask is to be transferred to the second year, provided he passes the examinations.

In 1914, the Finnish Annual Conference took place in the city of Helsinki from August 27 to 30. The records of the conference only reveal that Martin Prikask is a probationary member of the conference and is to be transferred to the second year of his studies. No list of appointments for the Russia Mission is included in the records of this year.

In 1915 the Finnish Annual Conference met in Gammalkarleby (Kokkola, in Finnish). In the report of the annual conference Martin Prikask appears in the list of ordained deacons of the Russia Mission. In section 24 it states that he is transferred to his third year of studies, accepted as a full member of the Conference and approved in his ordination as deacon. Again, no list of appointments is included.

In 1916 we find Martin Prikask among the 21 elders of the Finnish Annual Conference which took place in Ekenäs (Tammisaari, in Finnish). From the list of appointments in the 1916 year book, we see Prikask listed for the area of Arensburg (Kuressaare). Later we read that he has passed the required exams in the Russia Mission and has been approved for ordination as an elder. However no ordination is actually mentioned. The chaos of World War I, the fact that Prikask was effectively a member of two Conferences (Finnish and Russian) and the lack of surviving records from the Russia Mission, all contribute to complicate the situation.

Retired Finnish Superintendent, Tapani Rajamaa, discovered a record in the 1919 year book of the Methodist Episcopal Church in Finland, stating that Martin Prikask was ordained an elder in Tallinn on August 17, 1919 by Bishop Nuelsen, three years after he is listed among the elders in 1916.

World War I which started in 1914 made it difficult to hold annual conferences and those of 1915 and 1916 were chaired by Superintendent Simons. Presumably, Bishop Nuelsen was unable to attend due to the war, and so Prikask was listed among the elders starting in 1916, even though it would be three years before his formal ordination would be possible.

THE WAR OF INDEPENDENCE

During World War I when Superintendent George A. Simons was temporarily forced to leave Europe, Martin Prikask continued to lead the work of The Methodist Episcopal Church in Estonia. It was a troubled time for all of Europe.

For Estonia, the troubles that were to follow were the latest chapter in a very long story.[6] Since the year 1227, Estonians had lived under foreign rule of Germans, Swedes, and, since 1721, Imperial Russia. But with the collapse of the Russian Empire during the Bolshevik Revolution of 1917, Estonians claimed the freedom they had been dreaming of for 700 years. On February 24, 1918, Estonia declared its independence, a move that would not go unchallenged. From 1918 through 1920, the fledgling Estonian state had to fight both the armies of the German Empire and Russia's new Bolshevik regime in Estonia's War of Independence.

With the help of 3,000 Finnish, Swedish, and Danish volunteers, and with the British Royal Navy providing equipment and preventing a Russian naval assault, Estonia's makeshift army of farmers and students proved that men fighting for the freedom of their homes and families can accomplish the impossible. The last German army was defeated by advancing Estonian forces in northern Latvia near the city of Cēsis in June 1919, seven months after Germany surrendered to the Western allies, officially ending World War I. Finally, on February 2, 1920, the Tartu Peace Treaty was signed between the Republic of Estonia and Lenin's Bolshevist Russia in which Russia renounced all claims to the territory of Estonia for all eternity. The fact that Estonia was able to defeat both German and Russian forces is a testimony to how united Estonians were in the desire for independence.[7]

---

[6]   This section on Estonian history contributed by Mark & Kai Nelson.

[7]   As in many countries in the first decades of the 20th century, a considerable number of Estonians played with communism as a possible solution to the social problems they were facing. However, by 1918, Estonian interest in communism had plummeted due in part to a realization that the communist party would never support independence from Russia. When the War of Independence broke out, Estonian Bolsheviks did fight beside Russian Bolsheviks to establish a communist government in Estonia. Had this party been of any size, however, or had any amount of popular support, it would have easily fractured the small Estonian population so as to make victory in the War of Independence impossible. Interest in communism continued

With victory in the War of Independence, the Estonian Republic was able to develop as a sovereign, democratic, and capitalist nation. In the 1920's, land reforms reduced the size of the massive German-owned estates on which Estonians had worked as slaves until 1861. This land was then distributed to the local population, and Estonia became a country of small family farms. Improving social and economic security gave rise to a baby boom in the 1920's and 1930's that remains today as the largest demographic group, a living testimony to the hope and prosperity Estonia enjoyed during this all-too-brief period of freedom.

Sadly, we do not have a great deal of evidence concerning how Estonian Methodist leadership responded to these monumental events. What we do see is that the work of the church continued to grow despite the war.

In 1917, Prikask and his wife had to leave the island of Saaremaa and live temporarily in the capital city of Tallinn. They stayed with Johannes Laar, a fellow Christian and member of the Evangelical Christian Church. Later these two men, Martin Prikask and Johannes Laar, would become the two best-known figures in the Estonian Alliance movement. In the end of September of the same year, just weeks before the Bolshevik Revolution, Prikask traveled to Russia and worked for a brief period in the area of Volossovo, near the railway in the Peterhof district where many Estonians worked, especially in the summer.

In 1918, following the German occupation of the island of Saaremaa, Prikask was unable to return to his home church in Kuressaare. Consequently, in the month of January he settled down on the western coast of the Estonian mainland, in the city of Haapsalu. Shortly after, on March 9, 1918, he founded

---

to drop in the years that followed; and so, on the eve of the Soviet annexation of Estonia, documents show the Estonian communist party having a membership of a mere 150 people.

Martin and Liisi Prikask in 1922.

the Haapsalu congregation of The Methodist Episcopal Church in Estonia with 16 original members (4 men and 12 women). The newly founded congregation met in the residence of August Mikkov, on Ehte Street 7, and here Prikask served communion for the first time. The Haapsalu congregation was officially registered only in 1920 as an affiliate of the Kuressaare congregation.

While the War of Independence continued to rage, Martin Prikask drew up the first constitution of The Methodist Episcopal Church in Estonia, which was legally recognized on September 23, 1919, by the Tallinn-Haapsalu magistrate and registered under entry no. 169 in the Registry of Societies and Associations. The original title of the document published in Kuressaare in 1920, was "Methodist Episcopal Congregation in Estonia." According to article 7 of the constitution, the location of the congregation was the city of Kuressaare or the capital city of Estonia, Tallinn, or elsewhere, should such need arise. Article 16 stipulated that the Methodist Episcopal Congregation of Estonia had a right to plant new congregations as affiliates anywhere within the borders of the Republic of Estonia. New affiliates could be founded on the application of ten individuals. In essence, it was a church hierarchy with its own central body (in this case the main congregation in Kuressaare) under which there was subordination of congregations (at the time called affiliates). It is a great testimony to the vision and faith of Prikask and the other Estonian Methodist leaders that, even before the war was won, they were planning for the future. Despite the tremendous turmoil in politics and society they kept their vision and their purpose as men who knew their divine calling.

BETWEEN THE TWO WORLD WARS

January of 1921 saw a major spiritual revival begin in the Sõrve peninsula (the southwestern tip of the island of Saaremaa), as a result of which in 1924 churches were founded in Torgu and Pöide (the latter had its administrative location in the village of Keskvere, present-day Kõrkvere) as affiliates of the Kuressaare congregation.

The first district conference[8] of The Methodist Episcopal Church in Estonia took place from July 27 to 31, 1921, in the city of Haapsalu. It is noteworthy that Jaak Kukk, the bishop of the Estonian Evangelical Lutheran Church, allowed the Methodists to use the Haapsalu cathedral for the worship service during the conference. It was at this conference that Bishop John L. Nuelsen appointed Martin Prikask as the superintendent of the Estonian district with an office to be located in Tallinn.

As superintendent, he immediately sought opportunities to establish new congregations. For this purpose two houses were purchased in Tallinn, located at Suur-Pärnu Street 19 and 21, for worship services and children's work respectively. The Tallinn Methodist Episcopal Congregation was established on March 3, 1922. In addition to Superintendent Prikask, two others who were instrumental in the founding of the new congregation were from St. Petersburg, Superintendent George A. Simons and Dr. Vladimir Rafalovsky. The original list of congregation members included 3 men and 4 women, but the church grew rapidly

---

[8] Martin Prikask himself uses the phrase "Annual Conference"; however, at this time Estonia was not a full-fledged annual conference according to the Methodist Episcopal system. Only in 1929 would a Baltic Annual Conference be formed, covering not just Estonia, but Latvia and Lithuania as well.

and by the end of the year they counted 45 members in the congregation. In 1923, there were 82 members and by 1924, 109 members were reported. Martin Prikask was in charge of leading the congregation until September 1922, when it was entrusted to Ferdinand Tombo. Quite early on the congregation branched out in two new affiliations. One of these affiliates was in Nissi, where Vilhelm Meinvald was appointed to serve. The second, however, in Harju-Madise, struggled with low attendance.

Martin Prikask (front row, center left) together with Eduard Raud and the confirmation class in the Kuressaare church in 1923.

In 1922, the position of district superintendent was abolished and Prikask was appointed as the Secretary for the Mission. During the same year, the Kuressaare congregation invited him back to Saaremaa. In Kuressaare, together with Eduard Raud as his co-worker, he was active until 1923. As a result, the congregation in Kuressaare grew to the point that the church building became too small to accommodate all the parishioners. Consequently, in 1923 the church building was expanded by about 18 feet (6 meters), one third of its original length. After leaving Saaremaa, Prikask worked in Haapsalu (1923–1924), again in Kuressaare

(1924–1931), and from time to time also in Kõrkvere (1926–28), Tallinn (1932–1933), and then again in Kuressaare (1933–1941).

The Mission's conference of 1924, held in Kuressaare and chaired by Dr. Anton Bast, was historically significant for two reasons. Firstly, the conference was renamed as the Baltic and Slavic Mission Conference. Secondly, Aleksander Kuum, a future Superintendent, was accepted as a probationary member.

In 1924, when Martin Prikask celebrated his 50th birthday, the Methodist magazine *Kristlik Kaitsja (Christian Advocate)* gave the following evaluation of his spiritual work:

"70 brothers are working under the leadership of Martin Prikask. Every year they come together in Kuressaare for a few days for lectures given by pastor Prikask in which he gives them various tips on successful evangelization. Also in the same manner he holds short courses on the same subject for women. In the rural areas during the years of his activity, many a church has been erected and over one hundred points of evangelization have been established. Under his leadership Methodism has spread across Saaremaa and therefore the island can proudly call herself 'an island of Methodists.' Likewise, he has founded many congregations across Estonia and his work has been greatly blessed."(Kristlik Kaitsja, 1927, p.188)

Everything written in this article bears great witness to Martin Prikask's dedication to God.

On August 30, 1932, Martin Prikask went to Tallinn and worked in the first congregation at Veerenni Street 4A. Whenever possible, Prikask visited the second Tallinn congregation in the Kopli district, which was led by Pastor Ferdinand Tombo. God had blessed the work of the Methodist brothers: people were frequenting the worship services and God's Holy Spirit was at work in people's hearts. The work growing, Prikask felt it was time to return to Kuressaare the very next year.

In early 1935, a new constitution of The Methodist Episcopal Church in Estonia was drawn up, stipulating the autonomy of the Methodist church in Estonia. The new constitution placed Prikask in the position of acting bishop until the next annual conference. This conference, which took place September 7–10, 1935, in Tallinn, unanimously elected Prikask as superintendent in the capacity of bishop. His candidacy had been previously approved by the Act of the Head of State, a legal requirement of the time. This turn of events was not an act of rebellion against the episcopal leadership of the day, Bishop Raymond J. Wade; rather it was a move necessitated by Estonian law that required religious groups to have their leader inside the territory of the Republic of Estonia. The Methodist Episcopal Church in Estonia and Superintendent Prikask remained faithful to Bishop Wade, even if the law of the land did not allow this to be formalized in the constitution.

As of January 1940, the total membership of The Methodist Episcopal Church in Estonia reached 1836 members in 14 registered congregations: Tallinn First, Tallinn Second, Haapsalu, Tapa, Rakvere, Paide, Tartu, Viljandi, Pärnu, Narva, Avanduse, Kuressaare, Torgu, and Põide.

The last annual conference chaired by Martin Prikask was held in the Tallinn Second Congregation, February 23–25, 1940. In addition to Superintendent Prikask, the following members were elected to the Church Board: Aleksander Kuum, Martin Kuigre, Harri Uuetoa, Johannes Klementi, and Valdo Ojassoo. Many amendments were passed at the annual conference, including changes to the constitution of the church and the responsibilities of the church departments. As well, the name of the church was officially changed to *Eesti Metodisti Kirik* (Estonian Methodist Church or EMC)[9].

---

[9] This remains the legal name of the church in Estonian. With the formation of

On Estonian Independence Day (February 24), celebrated during the annual conference, the theme of the worship service held in the Tallinn Second Congregation was "What is needed at present, in my opinion." From many speeches that were held, Martin Prikask's words were the ones that sank in to people's memory: "We need silent prayer and concentration in order to gain victorious and active power (of the Holy Spirit)." (*Kiriku peakoosolek*, 1940:58-59.) These words were uttered at a time when over the country's political horizon dark clouds were forming.

After August 1940, the *Kristlik Kaitsja* magazine did not appear in print. World War II had started. In the entry of Prikask's home there hung a symbolic picture: a large clock at five minutes before midnight. Under the clock it red: "Behold, I Come Swiftly." It did not take long before it struck midnight for Martin Prikask. He was taken away, far away to Siberia and from there taken home by his Shepherd.

PUBLIC LIFE

Martin Prikask was actively involved in many charities. In 1921, he was elected a lifetime member of the Estonian Red Cross. He acted as the vice-chairman in the Saaremaa committee of the Estonian Red Cross, also as a trustee of the Estonian Temperance Movement. Prikask was on the board of two banks, the Kuressaare branch of the Bank of Estonia, as well as the Union Bank of the Islands. From 1920 to 1930 he was Kuressaare city councilman and between 1925 and 1927, chairman of the city council. Throughout Estonia's period of independence he was

---

the worldwide United Methodist Church in 1968, the official English name would become The United Methodist Church in Estonia. For this book, the name Estonian Methodist Church or EMC will be used for events between 1940 and 1968. (Translator's note)

also a member of the *Vaestelastekohus*, the court that dealt with the adoption of children.

When Martin Prikask fell ill on April 15, 1935, the local newspaper *Meie Maa* immediately ran an article on his health and expressed hope that he would get well soon. This incident shows how very loved and respected he was as a Christian among the islanders. In fact, due to his many good contacts abroad his reputation traveled far beyond Estonia's borders.

Prikask's active role in both the spiritual as well as the secular sphere was recognized by the Estonian authorities. On February 24, 1938, he was decorated by the president with the national order of the Estonian Red Cross, 3rd class, awarded for outstanding humanitarian service.

CHRISTIAN PUBLICATION

Martin Prikask was also a prolific writer. He authored many articles, Christian books, and acted as the chief editor for a Christian magazine. In 1919, he assisted in publishing a family magazine called *Kristlik Perekonna Leht* in Tallinn. The experience gained in Tallinn was instrumental in launching the publication of a Methodist magazine in Kuressaare, called *Kristlik Kaitsja*, in May of 1920. The magazine gained its name from an American church magazine called *The Christian Advocate*. From September 1923, the publishing of the magazine was entrusted to Hans Söte in Tallinn. After Söte immigrated to Germany, the chief editor's position went back to Prikask in Kuressaare in September, 1928. For the first three months the magazine was printed under the name *Uus Kristlik Kaitsja (The New Christian Advocate)*; however, from December the following issues were under the old name. A new editor was appointed in May 1933, Aleksander Kuum from Tartu. Due to the war he was forced to stop the publishing of the magazine. The last issue was published in June/July 1940.

Between 1935 and 1936, Kuressaare Methodist Congregation published a magazine called *Koduteel*, with Martin Prikask as the executive editor. The first issue of the magazine was launched on February 28, 1935, and it became the periodical for all the Saaremaa congregations. Since May 1990, The UMC in Estonia has been publishing a magazine under the same name once again.

Martin Prikask authored 12 books, the best known of which is *Neli usuelu astet (Four Steps in the Life of Faith)*, which reveals the clarity of the author's spiritual vision. In addition to being a brilliant writer, he also translated many books. Most prominent of which was undoubtedly *The Catechism of the Methodist Episcopal Church*, by W. Nast. Prikask also wrote many forewords, commentaries, song lyrics, and articles for various periodicals.

TURNING TIDES AND SUFFERING IN SIBERIA

For nineteen years after the Tartu Peace Treaty in which Soviet Russia pledged to respect Estonia's territorial integrity for all eternity, the Republic of Estonia and The Methodist Episcopal Church in Estonia flourished.[10] But it was not to last. On August 23, 1939, on the very eve of World War II, the Molotov-Ribbentrop Pact, also known as the German-Soviet Non-aggression Pact, was signed in Moscow. However, what was not known at the time was that the pact included a secret protocol that divided the nations of northern and eastern Europe into German and Soviet spheres of influence, a clear violation of the Tartu Peace Treaty. This secret protocol was only revealed after Germany's defeat in 1945 when the Western allies discovered the documents within the archives of the Third Reich.[11]

---

[10] This section on Estonian history contributed by Mark & Kai Nelson.

[11] The discovery of the secret protocols was a great embarrassment of the Soviet Union, which resolutely refused to recognize their existence until the Supreme Soviet of the USSR both admitted and repudiated them in a resolution signed by Mikhail Gorbachev on December 24, 1989.

ПРИНКАСК.МАРТИН РИТСОВИЧ 1877.г

The very last photograph of Martin Prikask, taken following his arrest in 1941.

The secret protocol of 1939, in clear violation of the Tartu Peace treaty, implicitly called for *"territorial and political rearrangements"* in the areas of Finland, Estonia, Latvia, Lithuania, Poland, and Romania. In keeping with this agreement, each of these countries was invaded, occupied, and forced to cede part or all of its territory to either the Soviet Union, Germany, or both.

On September 1, 1939, barely a week after the Nazi-Soviet pact had been signed, the partition of Poland commenced with the German invasion. The Soviet Union, true to the terms of their agreement with Hitler, then invaded Poland from the east on September 17. Stalin continued to move quickly with an efficiency that betrays a carefully laid plan. On September 28, Estonia was forced to sign a so-called Defense and Mutual Assistance Pact, which permitted the Soviet Union to establish military bases holding 25,000 soldiers in western Estonia (the entire standing army of the Republic of Estonia at the time consisted of only 15,000 men). Within days, a similar pact was forced upon Latvia and Lithuania. Moscow insisted that this was necessary to protect these countries from German aggression, a claim that would eventually be revealed as pure deception when the secret protocols of the Molotov-Ribbentrop Pact would come to light.

Death certificate of Martin Prikask.

Claiming they were planning to break their agreement, the Soviet Union's next step was to totally occupy Estonia and

Latvia on June 17, 1940. The very same day, a socialist coup was organized in Lithuania, which had been occupied by Soviet forces several days earlier. On June 21, similar coups were staged in Estonia and Latvia, with every event in this choreographed drama deliberately arranged to give the impression of public support for abandoning independence. Documents remaining from the time period show that there was indeed an Estonian Communist Party active and very much involved in supporting the Soviet takeover. The same documents also show that membership of the Estonian Communist Party immediately before these events was a mere 150 individuals.

The stage was now set for the next act: elections, held in all three countries on July 14 and 15. Like all Soviet elections before or since, only communist candidates were allowed to stand and like all Soviet elections, the result was predetermined to reflect the will of Moscow, regardless of the will of the people. Finally, at the request of the newly "elected" governments, on August 3, Lithuania, followed by Latvia on August 5 and Estonia on August 6, 1940, were formally annexed by the Soviet Union. The farcical drama had reached its climax, and the freedom that had been won just two decades earlier, was lost.[12]

In the years of terror that followed the Soviet occupation of the three Baltic countries, the newly annexed border regions were ethnically cleansed. In Estonia this would be most severe in the

---

[12] One of the more absurdly comical events in this tragedy occurred in February 1946, when three separate letters arrived at the offices of the League of Nations from the new Soviet governments of the three Baltic States. The letters requested that assets belonging to the independent republics of Estonia, Latvia, and Lithuania be transferred to the Soviet Union, since these countries had chosen to join the USSR. What is almost comical is that all three letters are written in Russian and are word for word identical. (The letters remain in the State Archives of Great Britain and are documented in the unpublished Ph.D. dissertation of Vahur Made, University of Tartu, 1999.)

northeastern region around the city of Narva. Across the length and breadth of the Baltic countries, the local population was purged of "anti-Soviet elements," meaning any individual with the potential to be a leader against the Soviet regime. This included anyone who was politically or socially active, businessmen, teachers, doctors, clergy, and well-to-do farmers. Tens of thousands of people were executed and hundreds of thousands of men, women, and children were deported to Siberia or sent to GULAG corrective labor camps[13], where many perished.

The Prikask headstone at the Kudjape Cemetery
(photo from the archive of Saaremaa Museum).

We can only imagine what went through the minds of the Methodist leadership as they saw these events unfold. The first mass deportation on Estonian territory in June of 1941, spared

---

[13] The GULAG, a Russian acronym for "Main Directorate for Corrective Labor Camps," had several million inmates. Prisoners included murderers, thieves, and other common criminals, along with political and religious dissenters. The GULAG, whose camps were located mainly in remote regions of Siberia and the Far North, made significant contributions to the Soviet economy in the period of Joseph Stalin by providing slave labor for large-scale projects from mining to building canals and railways.

Martin Prikask. However during the second wave of deportations, which took place just a month later, on July 1, 1941, Prikask and his wife were among many Saaremaa residents seized and taken initially to Tallinn. However, the attack of Nazi Germany upon the Soviet Union just days earlier on June 22, in clear violation of their mutual nonaggression pact, had caught the Soviet Red Army totally unprepared. In turn this created chaos in the whole of the Soviet transportation system. For the Prikasks, it meant that the Soviet authorities could not successfully complete the deportation on the original scale. Nevertheless, the men were still sent to Siberia, whereas women and children, including Liisi Prikask, were let go after a brief imprisonment in Tallinn. Martin Prikask was deported together with Saaremaa pastors Peeter Häng (from Torgu) and Vassili Prii (from Kõrkvere) far away from their home to distant Siberia.

Among the prosecution's documents against Prikask is one signed by Senior Lieutenant Tihhomirov of the People's Commissariat for Internal Affairs, or the NKVD for short (predecessor of the KGB), stating that the accused Prikask, formally arrested on August 8, 1941, is being detained in the Aleksandrovsk prison in the Irkutsk *oblast* (administrative district), which lay in southeastern Siberia near the border of Mongolia, more than 6,000 kilometers (4,300 miles) from his home on Saaremaa! The document also states that there is no evidence against him: "lack of evidence of the case of crime," Soviet legal jargon that effectively said, "a crime is considered to have been committed, but unfortunately we cannot prove it." In 1994, the state archives of newly re-independent Estonia gave Kuressaare congregation member Arvi Lindmäe copies of documents, revealing that the last interrogation of Martin Prikask took place on March 19, 1942, in the city of Irkutsk, where he was held in custody. The kangaroo court, the NKVD *troika* –

a three-person commission used in the Soviet Union for quick judgments during Stalin's reign of red terror – was presided over by the very same Senior Lieutenant Tihhomirov. The verdict was a foregone conclusion: death sentence for the prisoner. Prikask was accused of anti-Soviet activity and being active as a preacher in a religious sect. By order No. 001618 of the NKVD of the Soviet Union, dated November 21, 1941, the matter was given over to the special hearing of the Peoples Commissary for a final ruling.

Not until August 12, 1942, did this cruel special hearing came to a unanimous sentence: "Prikask Martin, son of Rits – execution by shooting" signed, Ivanov. Martin's father's name was actually Frits, a totally foreign name for the Russian officers involved. As a result, the order of execution mistakenly refers to Prikask by the Russian expression "Ritsovitch" meaning, "son of Rits." It is ironic that both Martin Prikask's birth and his death are recorded in foreign languages, his birth in the Halliste church records in German, and his death in Russian. Sadly, neither had the basic human decency to spell his name correctly, a sad comment on the times in which Martin Prikask lived and died.

The next entry in Martin Prikask's dossier is from September 9, 1942: "sentence carried out." This is the last entry. The death certificate, issued on November 30, 1990, by the civilian registry office in Kuressaare, confirms that the execution took place by the order of the NKVD in Aleksandrovsk, Irkutsk *oblast*. The death sentence of the court-martial was legally based on the §58-10, which referred to anti-Soviet propaganda, including religious activity. On his death certificate the spelling of his name is standardized to "Priikask," which explains why the Bureau of the Estonian Registry of the Repressed as well as the database of the Kistler-Ritso Estonia Foundation, which runs the Museum of Occupations in Tallinn, spells his name in the similar fashion. Prikask himself always spelled his surname with only one "i."

The location of martyr Prikask's grave remains unknown. Nonetheless, on the island of Saaremaa in Kudjape Cemetery, on the grave of his wife Liisi Prikask (who died in 1960) stands a headstone engraved as a memorial to Superintendent Prikask.

The undying memory of Martin Prikask will always remain at the very heart of the story of The Methodist Church in Estonia as well as in the hearts of the Methodist brothers and sisters who were guided by him to our Savior Lord Jesus.

Many years later, a handful of Christian brothers from his church in Kuressaare traveled all the way to Irkutsk, bringing with them a memorial stone from his homeland, to place as a commemorative marker at the last resting place of our first superintendent and martyr. They stood in mournful reverence and spent time in prayer.

Martin Prikask, we shall meet again at the Great Dawn!

Remembering Martin Prikask

Martin Prikask in 1917.

I would like to add the following episodes of Martin Prikask's life as they have been recorded by a pastor of the Kuressaare Methodist Congregation, Johannes Truu (1907–1999). Truu met Prikask at the age of 18 and soon became a member of the congregation and an active co-worker. He went on to serve as pastor of the same congregation from 1970 to 1976. The following text has been edited and abridged from its original, handwritten version, dating from 1976.

First Encounter

Nearby my childhood home in Saaremaa prayer meetings were held in one of the farmhouses. As it had been a popular place for village dances, the young people were not intimidated to gather there for the meetings. Having a prayer meeting was quite unheard of in those days. Furthermore, the gospel had never been preached in those parts of the countryside. I sat quite boldly in the front row. Three men sat in the front, two were older, but the younger one was an acquaintance of mine. Accompanied by a guitar, a young woman sang about the prodigal son. I felt the song strike a chord in my heart. Already at the first meeting I felt an urge to go, like the prodigal son in the song, back to the Father. However, that actually happened a couple of weeks later. I was 18 years old. Only sometime later did I discover that Martin Prikask was the author of that song. Therefore, I can say, that my first meeting with Martin Prikask was through a song.

FIRST IMPRESSIONS

Liisi and Martin Prikask in 1916.

Upon entering the Kuressaare Methodist Church, one man in particular immediately caught my attention. With a joyful smile he had a way of winning everybody over without uttering a single word. He was modest in his manners and sincere. I felt at once that this was a true man of God, worthy of my friendship and trust. Not long after, I applied to join the congregation. This was an extraordinary day in my life. I remember how I was directed to go to the adjacent room, right next door from the church hall, while the brothers decided upon accepting me into membership. Then I was called back and asked many questions, which I had to answer. Afterwards all the brothers came to me and congratulated me as a new member of the congregation. From this day on, I started my co-operation with the church. As a younger brother I was made useful in the choir and in the pulpit. My father had passed away the same year and now God became my Father. Brother Prikask could also be called a true father (although Prikask and his wife had no children of their own). He was an educated man, but at the same time a simple common man, like the rest of us.

BROTHER PRIKASK'S WORSHIP SERVICES

In the countryside, the worship services were always crowded. Both children and the elderly could plainly understand his meaning. He never spoke idle words. His sermons were consistent, clear, and memorable. He spoke on sanctification, spiritual growth, work of the Holy Spirit. Sometimes he explained the Scripture word for word, other times he preached repentance – a true evangelical message. It was always effective, because the seeds that he sowed, in most cases, fell on good soil and bore fruit manyfold.

I particularly remember one sermon on the ten virgins. It was so vivid and effective, that the listeners were in tears.

PERSONAL EXAMPLE

Prikask was always neatly dressed. He wore a white stiff collar that gave a very clerical impression. Although a superintendent, I do not recall him flaunting a big cross and chain. He loved to visit the rural areas accompanied by his wife and it was ever so pleasant to see them. In the countryside, farmhouses were oftentimes like hospital wards, where Brother Prikask would be seen praying for the ill and dying.

My wife, who grew up in the village of Lümanda, spoke of how in the cold winter time Prikask had to come on horse-drawn sleigh. But at times even the sleigh could not get through, so he had to trudge on foot through deep snow in order to make it to the Lümanda service. He did not have the modern comforts of transportation we have today. On a rare occasion he was able to use a bus to transport people. Nonetheless, the worship services were particularly blessed and people were saved at almost every meeting.

The hall of the Kuressaare Methodist church, ready to receive guests.

CONGREGATIONAL DISCIPLINE

People accepted as members of the congregation had to have a very clear testimony of their conversion. People who did not have clear assurance of their salvation were not easily accepted as members of the church. If such was the case, the applicant was to go back and spend time in prayer, in order to return with a renewed heart. These people usually brought a new blessing into the church. Brother Prikask did not allow anyone to the pulpit who had missed out two Communions without a compelling reason. He also denied participating in Holy Communion to anyone who had committed a mistake that was in grave violation of the vow taken before the congregation. That person had to sort the problem out as soon as possible. Excommunication was quite a common occurrence, and usually these ex-members came back with tears of repentance and were accepted back in the congregation.

Services always started on time. When the clock struck, the organ started to play. I can not remember even one service when brother Hark, or in his absence, brother Prikask, were not seated at the organ on the dot.

Brothers who were preaching, were to remain within the passage and preach the Word without getting off topic. The speaker had to be appropriately and neatly dressed, the same was asked of the members of the choir.

ALL THINGS TO ALL MEN

Brother Prikask was all things to all men. He played a needed role in both the Kuressaare city council and in the Bank of Estonia. He was a businessman and he kept livestock. He was a very versatile man. I heard someone comment once how blessed his ministry would have been if he kept all his eggs in the same basket. Maybe that person was right. But, if that had been the case, we would never have gotten our first church building, since that came from Martin Prikask's personal commitment and generous offering, which was only possible because of his business involvement.

IN THE MIDST OF GOD'S WORK

Martin Prikask had won the trust of the islanders and bound them to him through love. The work of the church expanded and the congregation grew day-by-day. The Methodist work started in 1907, the same year I was born. Every year in the middle of October there was an all-Estonian Methodist conference held in Kuressaare. People came together from near and far, even from outside the Methodist congregation. These were unforgettable times. On the top floor of the church there was singing and praying all through the night. The church was packed and bursting at the seams. At half past seven there was a prayer meeting, at ten o'clock the worship service. At one o'clock we broke for lunch. At three o'clock and eight o'clock there were services. All in all four worship services were held and three meals served for some 400 people a day. On the Sunday evening of the conference, people were invited to stay for a follow-up service. There were people crowding to the front of the church following the altar call, it reminded me of the injured crowding into the military hospital. Brother Prikask had to admit that even using the adjacent room would not accommodate all the people who came forward for prayer. It was the Lord's work. Partially it was due to the lack of churches in the city. Besides the Lutheran church and a small free church, there were no places were believers could gather.

These are but mere fragments of my recollections of Martin Prikask. In conclusion I would like to say that Brother Prikask was a spirit-filled and anointed tool in the hands of the Lord.

JAAN JAAGUPSOO

(born Jakobson)
(July 14, 1898 – July 5, 1941)

We are hard pressed on every side, but not crushed; perplexed, but not in despair; persecuted, but not abandoned; struck down, but not destroyed. . . . For our light and momentary troubles are achieving for us an eternal glory that far outweighs them all. So we fix our eyes not on what is seen, but on what is unseen. For what is seen is temporary, but what is unseen is eternal.
2 Corinthians 4:8–9; 17–18

A photograph from 1930.

GOD'S BETTER PLANS

Jaan Jakobson (later Jaagupsoo)[14], was born on July 14, 1898. In the process of compiling this book, I was unable to establish either

---

[14] With a few exceptions, Estonians in the 1800's were given predominantly German and occasionally Swedish surnames by their foreign landlords. However, in the 1930's, under the independent Estonian Republic, it was made possible for people to

the place of his birth or the identity of his parents. In his younger years he resided 10 years in the city of Tartu where he worked at the university's Wound Care Clinic as a hospital orderly. By this point he had already been a believer for a few years. Although his pay and place of work were quite satisfactory, he still felt that he wanted to be financially more secure. In order to achieve this goal, he decided to move to North America. He had acquired all the necessary documents for the trip across the ocean except for one, a clean bill of health. The doctor could not declare Jaagupsoo fit as he was inflicted with septicemia in his left arm, which hung in a sling concealing a number of wounds that simply would not heal. Days became weeks, weeks became months.

However, God had other plans. Karl Kuum came to preach in Tartu with a message from God. Jaan, who sat in the front row with his infected arm in a sling, heard the Holy Spirit speak to him through Brother Karl Kuum's lips. The message was of God's faithfulness and God's promise to take care of him. Jaan gave up his plan to go to America and when he reached home that evening, he noticed the swelling in the arm had receded and the fever was gone. Overnight the arm was healed completely. Next day his arm was well enough that he could put on his Sunday best and attend the evening worship service. This experience was a powerful proof to Jaan that God could be trusted in every kind of hardship.

MINISTRY IN TARTU

Jaan Jakobson was appointed as a lay preacher to Tartu at the semi-annual meeting of the Baltic and Slavic Mission Conference in Riga, held January 26–28, 1927. At the annual conference of the Baltic and Slavic Mission held in Tallinn, August 28 –

Estonianize their names if they so chose. Jaan was born Jakobson, but in 1935 he had his last name officially changed to Jaagupsoo to make it sound Estonian. (Translator's note)

September 1, 1929, in the Methodist church on Veerenni Street, Jaan Jakobson was appointed as minister in the city of Tartu and surrounding area together with Aleksander Kuum. In addition to these clerical appointments he was elected as preacher for the Tartu Blue Cross (an organization that stemmed from the temperance movement) in 1930. With the endorsement of Aleksander Kuum, and as a result of Jakobson's preaching ministry, a second Tartu Methodist congregation emerged on March 1, 1931. At the annual conference of the Baltic and Slavic Mission in 1931 held in Tallinn, August 5–9, Jaan Jakobson was ordained as a deacon by Bishop Raymond J. Wade and consequently appointed to lead the work of the Tartu II congregation as well as in the nearby areas.

A photograph showing the Tartu II congregation. Jaan Jakobson sits in the center of the first row, holding his trumpet.

At the annual conference of the Baltic and Slavic Mission held in Riga, July 27–31, 1932, Jakobson was accepted as a full member of the annual conference and was reappointed to work in the Tartu II congregation. Altogether, Jakobson would work for three years at the Tartu II congregation, all the while preaching at the local Blue Cross, as well. Pastor Jakobson's diligent and self-sacrificing work bore abundant fruit. The fruit of this work was even seen in the music ministry of the Tartu II congregation and especially the brass band where pastor Jakobson played the trumpet.

In 1933, Bishop Wade ordained Jakobson as an elder at the Baltic and Slavic Annual Conference in Tallinn. The entire congregation watched the solemn ceremony with mixed feelings as the bishop, along with several other brothers, held out their hands and gave him their blessing. From now on Jakobson was to be appointed to serve in Haapsalu.

MINISTRY IN HAAPSALU CONGREGATION

On October 5, 1933, Jaan Jakobson left the Tartu II congregation for his new place of ministry in the city of Haapsalu, where he served as a pastor until his death in July 1941.

The engagement party held in Haapsalu August 19, 1934. At the table are seated, side-by-side, from left to right: Aleksander Kuum, Irene, and Jaan.

When Aleksander Kuum and Richard Järv, the editors of the *Kristlik Kaitsja (Christian Advocate)* magazine, visited him in

Haapsalu congregation in January of 1934, they could see that through Jakobson's efforts the church had come to new life. The evangelical meetings were always crowded and even on Sunday mornings he was preaching to a full house. The demand of the day had also turned him into a quite decent organist and choir conductor. He was actively participating in the ministry of the affiliated churches, and as a result of his diligence many inactive members found their way back to the Methodist church. The congregation along with the church youth presented him with a bicycle, in order that he would have an easier time getting around to all the churches in the area. Once settled in the city of Haapsalu, he made a point of visiting each church at least once per quarter.

On Sunday, August 19, 1934, a special celebration was arranged as Pastor Jaan Jakobson and Irene Lemberg, an elementary school teacher from the neighboring county of Noarootsi, were engaged to be married. Irene's parents, Gustav and Maria, lived in the village of Hosby near the local church.[15] Superintendent Martin Prikask married Jaan and Irene on October 7, 1934, following the Sunday evening worship service. The happy couple received many felicitations via mail as well as telegraph. But the eager servant of God did not take time off even for a honeymoon. Two days after his wedding he traveled to the island of Saaremaa where he preached in the local congregations of Muhu, Kõrkvere, Kuressaare, and Torgu. His visits left a long-lasting impression on the believers.

---

[15] The Noarootsi area near Haapsalu, together with most of Estonia's islands, was settled by Swedes starting in the 13th century. Referred to in Estonian as "Costal Swedes" (Rannarootslased) or in Swedish Aibofolke (a poetic expression meaning "Island People"), they maintained their language and cultural identity for 650 years, living as freemen during centuries in which Estonians were in serfdom. The Costal Swedes made their livelihood as simple fishermen and farmers, and always maintained warm relations with the Estonians. Irene Jaagupsoo's family was ethnically Swedish, a fact that will become very relevant. (Translator's note)

Jaan, Irene, and little Anne.

On April 16, 1935, Jaan Jakobson officially changed his surname to Jaagupsoo, to render it more Estonian-sounding, as was popular among Estonians in the 1930's.

In the spring of 1935, Jaagupsoo visited Hiiumaa, the second largest island in Estonia, where he held a number of spiritual meetings in various places with great success in terms of both attendance and response. Jaagupsoo described his evangelistic travels in the following account:

I brought back the best of impressions. However, I must point out that our Methodist work is still widely unknown on Hiiumaa. A couple of times I was approached by the heads of the families who expressed their apologies for being hesitant to let me preach there because they had never heard about these Methodists. But now they have invited me to come back soon and even tried to convince us to stay longer.

On a more personal note: October 20, 1936, was a joyous occasion for Jaan and Irene Jaagupsoo, as God blessed them with their firstborn daughter, Anne.

At the next annual conference of The Methodist Episcopal Church in Estonia, held in Tallinn's Petlemma Prayer Chapel on Sitsi Street, February 15-18, 1936, Jaan Jaagupsoo along with Peeter Häng and Karl Kösta were elected as members of the church's auditing committee. In the same year Jaagupsoo visited Finland in connection with the Epworth League's (EL) youth conference, preaching in the cities of Helsinki, Kuopio, Lahti, and Mikkeli, as well as Viipuri. In all of these places he received a warm welcome. One year later, at the XI youth conference of the Epworth League held in Tapa, Estonia (June 23–24, 1937), Jaagupsoo was elected to the board of the EL.

In the Haapsalu congregation in 1935. Seated in the front row, third from the left is Jaan Jaagupsoo, with his wife Irene sitting beside him. Beside Jan Jaagupsoo, second from the left, is Ferdinand Tombo, the pastor of Haapsalu congregation between 1926 and 1931.

Concerning his spiritual work in Haapsalu, one can say that the Methodist congregation had a favorable influence on the whole city. Haapsalu congregation cooperated with other free churches in the area. An ecumenical prayer group was founded that met on Thursday evenings in the smaller hall of the Methodist church. The group met with the purpose of renewing the personal sanctification of the individuals, interceding for a spiritual awakening among the people, and growth in the spirit of Christian ecumenicism. Beginning in the spring of 1936, weekly choir practices were held, bringing together singers from the Baptist, Methodist, and Moravian Brethren churches.

Jaagupsoo was an esteemed speaker who was frequently invited to preach all across Estonia. At the annual conference of the Baltic and Slavic Mission held in 1937 in Tartu, he was one of the main speakers for the missions evening. From the very beginning, The Methodist Church has been first and foremost a missionary church, and Jaagupsoo's heart for missions allowed God to use him in a very powerful way.

In 1938, when the Haapsalu congregation celebrated her 20th anniversary, the church had grown to include 350 members. Haapsalu daily *Lääne Elu* commented on the anniversary of the congregation, albeit with a puzzling error in the membership statistic quoted, in the following words:

"On March 13, the Haapsalu congregation of The Methodist Episcopal Church in Estonia celebrates the 20th anniversary of her birth. Haapsalu Methodist Congregation was founded on February 24, 1918.[16] The congregation was originally made up of 16 members with A. Mikkov as the first pastor and leader of the work. The services were held at various rented rooms at Ehte Street 7, Posti Street 17, Jaani Street 6. With aid from American Methodists, in four years time the congregation was able to build a church at 6 Endla Street, which was consecrated by bishop Dr. J. Nuelsen on July 23, 1922. Currently the membership stands at 320 people. The congregational board includes A. Mikkov, A. Paju, H. Teesalu, J. Iiling, J Prikk, J. Jaagupsoo. The pastor is J. Jaagupsoo."

Lääne Elu, "Metodisti Koguduse Juubel," 1938.

In the first half of 1939, God sent a spiritual awakening to the city of Haapsalu and to the village of Võnnu in the neighboring Ridala County. One cannot downplay the key role Jaagupsoo

---

[16] According to the Gregorian calendar the founding of Haapsalu congregation would have been on March 9, 1918, with 16 members. (Kristlik Kaitsja No 5/1936, p.79)

played in this revival by his methodical evangelizing and leading people in the villages to the Lord.

As a pastor, Jaagupsoo displayed an exceptional sense of Christian brotherhood and generosity toward fellow believers from other denominations. When the Haapsalu affiliate of the Evangelical Christian Union had to consider withholding public worship services due to lack of meeting rooms and being temporarily without a pastor, Jaagupsoo offered them the opportunity to use the rooms in the Methodist church for carrying on their work.

On October 2, 1939, Irene delivered their second daughter, Rutt.

But the good times were turning into times of testing. World War II was underway in Europe. The times were dark, and even blacker clouds were gathering on the horizon as Soviet troops were now on Estonian soil and Estonia's annexation into the Soviet Union was only months away.

The 1940 annual meeting of the Estonian Methodist Church was held February 23-25, in Tallinn's Petlemma Prayer Chapel. On February 24, Estonians would celebrate their Independence Day for what would prove to be the last time in half a century. On this day, a question was raised at the Methodist conference: "What does

The Jaagupsoo family residence in Haapsalu Methodist Church at no. 6 Endla Street.

Estonia need the most, right now?" The answer to this question constitutes Pastor Jaagupsoo's final recorded words, published in the April 1940 issue of the *"Kristlik Kaitsja" (Christian Advocate)* magazine. In his speech he simply said: "We must display more love in action."

VICTIM OF RED TERROR

World War II began with all its atrocities.

In the newly occupied regions of the Soviet Union, like Estonia, these were the times of Red Terror: special operations to eliminate the so-called "anti-Soviet elements" in society, including the clergy. Purges were carried out by the so-called Soviet destroyer battalions of the NKVD[17] with extreme ruthlessness. These destroyer battalions had free reign in their activities, which resulted in inhumane treatment of captives, regular use of torture, summary executions, as well as unwarranted and cruel treatment of the general public. People were frightened and distraught; nobody dared to speak out.

In hopes of escaping the Red Terror, Jaan Jaagupsoo took his family to the area of Noarootsi, to stay with his wife's parents. Mrs. Salme Kalm of Noarootsi, although only three years old at the time, remembers the Jaagupsoo family's arrival in the Hosby village, where Irene's parents lived. Irene and the children lived close to Salme's father's house, whereas Jaan, like many other good and decent men throughout these chaotic days, hid in the forest near Kudani village during the first part of July 1941. His wife Irene secretly took food to him in his hideout until one day her husband was nowhere to be found.

---

[17]   The NKVD was the Soviet secret police. The name would later be changed to the KGB. (Translator's note)

Rätsepa farmstead in the Hosby village, where Irene lived with her parents.

Earlier the same tragic year a third child was born to Jaan and Irene, a son, Jaan Jr, born April 2, 1941. He was barely three months old when his father was captured in the forest.

Concerning the death of Jaan Jaagupsoo there are somewhat differing accounts. In the book entitled, *Punane Terror* (Red Terror) by Mart Laar it is said that Jaagupsoo was murdered in a most sadistic way in the county of Noarootsi on Saturday, July 5, 1941 (1996, p. 188). The mutilated body of Jaagupsoo was discovered in a dry well by farmworkers making hay approximately half a kilometer from the forest, close to Kudani village. The preacher of the Moravian Brethren Church of the Haapsalu area, Evald Leps, told Dr. Heigo Ritsbek in an interview recorded on August 9, 1991, that when the body was identified, Irene came to see her husband. It was a terrible sight indeed: his eyes had been gouged out and his lifeless body bore marks of torture (Ritsbek 1993, p. 252).

One can only imagine the reaction of Haapsalu Methodist Congregation on the following Sunday when they heard the fate that had befallen their beloved pastor.

Finally, I will include the account by his eldest daughter Anne who, on the day of her father's murder, was not yet five years old and whose source of information is her mother's story. According to Anne, her father was missing for three days before his body was found thrown into a well. Her father had been shot from behind, the bullets hitting his midsection. Anne does not think her father was tortured before he was killed and that his eyes were intact. While Anne did manage to see the body when it was brought back to the house, it is questionable what she would have been allowed to see. Quite possibly her mother did not deem it necessary at the time to tell her young children the gory details of their father's death.

The Noarootsi Cemetery attendant Albert Rebane told in turn, that Jaagupsoo's body was found in a two-and-a-half-meter deep well that had sides lined with logs, located in a pasture near Kudani village. To cover their tracks, his executioners had thrown a tree stump on top of his body. On May 8, 2006, I ventured out in the company of Albert Rebane and Elmet Saupõld with a

The Noarootsi Cemetery attendant Albert Rebane pointing at the overgrown cattle well, into which the body of Jaan Jaagupsoo was disposed of. Photograph was taken on May 8, 2006.

mission to find the place where Jaagupsoo's body was discovered. We found a dense thicket growing in the former pasture. After a long and thorough search Albert Rebane managed to find the notorious well, although it was overgrown and had caved in over the years.

The headstone on the grave of Jaan Jaagupsoo at the Noarootsi Cemetery.

The wife of the Noarootsi Cemetery attendant, Lea Rebane, was only ten years old when she attended the funeral of Pastor Jaagupsoo. She remembers it was a beautiful summer day and a large crowd had gathered to pay their last respects to the deceased. Suddenly on the horizon there appeared trucks carrying the armed destroyer battalions with their latest prisoners. Just as the trucks reached the funeral procession, one of the detainees managed to jump off and make his escape by running into the forest. Immediately the armed guards opened fire in the direction of the fugitive. Miraculously he managed to get away, but in the course of shooting at the runaway, one of their own men was accidentally killed. Having witnessed this alarming scene, most people in the funeral procession turned back to the village in fear. As a result, apart from the immediate family members, the only person brave enough to stay for the funeral ceremony, was Leena Palmik, an aunt of Lea Rebane. Later it became public knowledge that on the day of Jaagupsoo's funeral, the destroyer battalion units shot eight people execution style in the area. Anne Jaagupsoo herself remembers hearing gunfire on the day of her father's funeral, however that is the extent of her recollections.

The earthly remains of Jaan Jaagupsoo are buried in the Noarootsi Cemetery (section IV, plot No. 417) beside his sister-in-law Adele (1903–1921) and mother-in-law Maria Lemberg (1881–1933).

In 1944, an agreement between the Swedish government and the German army, now in retreat from Estonia, allowed the Swedish residents of the Estonian islands and coastal areas to flee the returning Soviet forces across the Baltic Sea to Sweden. Among the many Swedes forced to leave the land that had been their home for nearly 700 years, was Jaagupsoo's wife Irene along with their three children. Starting the end of June, the schooners *Juhan* and *Tiina* made at least nine dangerous trips to Sweden before the Red Army arrived the beginning of September. Jaagupsoo's younger daughter Rutt wrote that she was onboard the schooner *Juhan* together with her mother, grandfather, sister Anne, and brother Jaan Jr. The Swedish Methodist Church looked after them, arranged a place for them to live and helped their mother find work. The family settled down in Alingsås, where Irene Jaagupsoo later remarried another Estonian refugee named Herman. Irene's father lived with them until his death in 1956. Irene herself went to be with the Lord in 1991 and was buried in Borås Cemetery beside her second husband. Her son Jaan Jr. (whom they began to call Jan), who currently resides in

Stenungsund, Sweden, restored his family's original Swedish name Jakobson. He visited his father's grave in Noarootsi, Estonia, in 2005. Daughter Rutt, who lives in Alingsås and whose married name is Wahlström, has also visited her father's grave. Both Rutt and Jaan Jr., are members of the Alingsås Methodist Church. The oldest daughter Anne, currently living in Uppsala, is also married and is a member of the Pentecostal Church.

To characterize Jaan Jaagupsoo, the words of a simple Noarootsi Swedish woman named Salme, ring true, "We have heard only good things about Jaan. He was an excellent and good father as well as very decent person."

We remember Jaan Jaagupsoo with the deepest gratitude and respect. He was a man who dedicated himself in his youth to the service of the kingdom of God and was willing to give his very life to the witness of Jesus Christ, staying true to him even until death. He lived to be not quite 43 years old.

Martyr for the Faith

Peeter Häng

(August 9, 1900 – September 21, 1942)

"His master replied, 'Well done, good and faithful servant! You have been faithful with a few things; I will put you in charge of many things. Come and share your master's happiness!'"
Matthew 25:21

Peeter Häng in the spring of 1933.

TEACHING IN TORGU ELEMENTARY SCHOOL

Peeter Häng was born August 9, 1900, on the island of Saaremaa, Torgu County, village of Hänga. As an infant he was christened in the Jämaja Lutheran church, where his parents held membership. His father, Jüri (1864–1957), was originally from Torgu County and his mother, Maria (born Ley, 1863–1951), came from the city of Kuressaare.

Mõntu Elementary School. In the front row, from left to right seated are the teachers Lydia and Peeter Häng, the school headmaster August Mälk, teacher Eduard Aru with pupils.

Materials from the Estonian historical archives give a detailed overview of his education and his becoming an elementary school teacher. Peeter studied three years at the Iide local school (1909–1912) and continued his education for another three years at the Torgu parish school. In 1917, he completed the summer course offered in the Estonian language by the Saaremaa School Teachers Association and, in 1918, the German language course taught in the city of Kuressaare. Between 1919 and 1921, he studied in Kuressaare, where the Ministry of Education arranged preparatory as well as advanced summer courses for teachers, allowing him to graduate as an elementary school teacher. Considering that much of this education took place during World War I, one can see how Peeter was able to skillfully use the possibilities available to him. In those troubled times it was extremely difficult to acquire a more solid education since nearly all the applied and general educational institutions were evacuated to Russia.

As early as the age of 16, he started as a substitute teacher at Iide School in Torgu (1916–1917) and later became a teacher at the Kaavi School (1917–1918). In 1918, the Board of Education appointed Peeter Häng as a teacher in the re-opened Kaunispäe School, where he worked until his army service in September of 1920. At the age of 20, Peeter enlisted in the army for a two-year term of service. Immediately after his release in September 1922, he was offered a teaching position in Torgu, where a new school was started at the local magistrate building. There he worked as a substitute teacher for grade 4 until the end of his term. In October of the same year, he was appointed as a substitute teacher at Türju School until March 1, 1923, when their regular teacher, Hermann, was well again. Then he was transferred to Mäepäe School until the end of his contract. On August 3, 1923, the parish council decided to elect three teachers to the Mõntu Elementary School. Of the candidates for the position, the following three were elected: Peeter Häng, Lydia Dsiss (the future wife of Peeter), and Eduard Aru. As a teacher Peter was able to teach Estonian, Russian, German, and English within the extent of the required programs for grades 1–3.

FAMILY MAN

Peeter's bride, Lydia Dsiss (October 22, 1903–September 29, 1960), came from Kuressaare. Her father, Issaak (1873–1916), was originally from the Kiev province in Ukraine, and her mother, Akulina (born 1876, maiden name Treimann), came from the Laimjala County of Saaremaa. Lydia was christened in the Kuressaare Apostolic Orthodox church of St. Nicolas where she was also a member. After her father's death, Lydia's mother lived in Nasva village near Kuressaare.

In 1922, following her graduation from Saaremaa High School in Kuressaare, Lydia started working as a teacher in Triigi

*Peeter and Lydia Häng in 1926 with
their firstborn daughter Leida.*

Elementary School in Leisi County. She also taught in the Mõntu school in Torgu County (from 1923 to 1932 and 1940 to 1942). Her later places of employment as a teacher and headmaster included Kaavi School (1932–1940) and Maantee Elementary (1942–1944).

Peeter Häng and Lydia Dsiss were married on September 21, 1924. The ceremony took place in the Torgu Apostolic Orthodox church and was performed by the local priest, Vassili Russ, and parish clerk, Konstantin Saar. One of Peeter's groomsmen, August Mälk, a colleague and a friend to Peeter and Lydia, later became known as a famous writer, who between 1923 and 1925 worked as the headmaster of the Mõntu school.

Once married, Peeter and Lydia lived in the village of Hänga in Torgu County. In 1925, the couple participated in the teacher's training summer courses for teachers of German language arranged by the University of Tartu.

On October 20, 1926, at ten o'clock in the morning, Lydia delivered a beautiful baby girl, whom they named Leida. She was born in the teacher's apartment in the Mõntu schoolhouse. Unfortunately, the infant contracted meningitis and died before she turned 18 months old. She died in the Kuressaare County hospital (or infirmary as it was commonly called back then) and was buried in the Jämaja Cemetery of the Lutheran church.

On September 14, 1929, at four o'clock in the afternoon, Lydia gave birth to their first son, George-Anatole (1929–1974), who was born in Kuressaare. At the time, the Häng family was residing in the Mõntu school building. Their second son, Louis (1930–1967), was born at the Mõntu schoolhouse on December 10, 1930, at half past nine in the morning.

For somewhat obscure reasons, Peeter Häng was fired from the Mõntu Elementary School on August 1, 1932. The reason given for his firing is the regulation on employment relations. To an uninformed bystander it seems that this decision was connected to Peeter Häng's appointment as a pastor to Torgu Methodist Congregation. From 1932 to 1936, Peeter Häng was able to serve the congregation in Torgu wholeheartedly and on a full-time basis. The *Kristlik Kaitsja (Christian Advocate)* magazine's editor wrote in his column that Häng decided to set himself apart for the service of the Lord.

Meanwhile the family continued to grow. Their third son, Leevi, was born in 1932 and now lives in Kuressaare (2006). Three years later, the couple had a fourth son, Johannes (1935–1984).

Between November 6 and May 11, 1939, Peeter substituted for his wife in Kaavi Elementary School, acting as teacher and director. The last time Peeter Häng was employed in a secular job was as a teacher's

Peeter and Lydia Häng with sons (from left to right): George-Anatole, Leevi, Johannes, and Louis.

assistant in Mõntu Elementary School, substituting for his wife from September 25 to October 3, 1940.

To sum up his teaching career, we may say that Peeter Häng worked in different elementary schools across Saaremaa, putting in full-time hours from October 15, 1916 to October 3, 1940, altogether some 14 years, 1 month, and 23 days.

While living in Kaavi, they had two daughters, Anni (1937–2005), Maira-Saima (1938, living in Russia at present, 2006), and a son, Heino-Joosua (1939–2004). Altogether they had eight children in their large family: five sons and three daughters, one of whom died in infancy. This information is given by Leevi Häng, who is currently living in Kuressaare and is 74 years old at the time of writing. Leevi reminisced: *When our family was seized for deportation in 1941, I was barely 9 years old. I remember from my childhood that our father was quite a disciplinarian, quite demanding and severe but just, a trait that was compensated by our mother's extremely mild and pampering attitude toward us children. By the time I was born, the former Mõntu elementary teacher had transformed into a pastor in the congregation.*

CO-WORKER OF KARL KUUM

In January of 1921, during Peeter Häng's military service, a spiritual revival movement began on the Sõrve peninsula of the island of Saaremaa. For this purpose God was able to use Eduard Raud, a man with a heart set on fire for God. When Eduard Raud established Torgu Methodist Congregation in 1924, Karl Kuum was appointed as leader for two years. Being an enterprising man, Karl Kuum started constructing a new church building. The festive cornerstone event was held on April 29, 1928; and in the same year, on October 28, the brand-new church building was consecrated by Superintendent Martin Prikask. It was on the exact same day sixteen years earlier that the very first Methodist

Episcopal Church building was consecrated in the city of Kuressaare.

Torgu Church under construction in the spring of 1928.

Peeter Häng has said that at the time of the construction of the Torgu church he was not yet a believer; however, in 1929, four years prior to Karl Kuum's death, it was the very same Brother Kuum who ushered him toward Christ. Peeter Häng expressed his heartfelt love and great dedication in his work in the Torgu congregation. Side by side with Karl Kuum they painted the interior of the church and put siding on the exterior. Peeter Häng became the faithful co-worker of Karl Kuum, one of the first preachers of The Methodist Episcopal Church in Estonia.

PASTOR OF THE TORGU METHODIST CONGREGATION

In 1932, Karl Kuum retired as the pastor of the Torgu congregation due to failing health. At the annual conference of the Baltic and Slavic Mission, held in Riga, the capital city of Latvia, July 27–31, 1932, Peeter Häng was ordained as a deacon and appointed to serve as pastor of the Torgu congregation.

Peeter Häng, having worked for years as a teacher in elementary schools, now decided to dedicate himself to serve the Lord. In August of 1939, even while participating in the teacher's courses held in Tartu, he helped out in the local congregation by preaching the gospel. As a preacher, he was welcome in many congregations and branches of The Methodist Church across Estonia.

In Torgu, Häng served with the aid of many loyal and energetic brothers. The church in Torgu had formerly been exposed to several waves of theologically controversial teachings, fortunately during Häng's ministry the situation normalized and such upheavals subsided. The focus was turned to salvation for sinners and the life of sanctification.

Torgu Methodist Episcopal Church in the fall of 1928.

Valdo Ojasoo, who visited the Torgu congregation on October 19, 1937, from the editor's office of the Estonian Methodist magazine *Kristlik Kaitsja (Christian Advocate)*, characterized the ministry of the congregation in the following words: *In Torgu we have a nice ministry. God has blessed the efforts of Kuum Senior in an awesome way. As a result of his work there stands a beautiful church under the pine trees with over 200 people in attendance. It should be emphasized that the church has been built without foreign aid and loans.* (Valdo Ojasoo, "Impressions from the Trip to Saaremaa." *Kristlik Kaitsja*, 1937, I p. 11)

At the end of September 1937, Peeter Häng traveled to England in order to take a training course for Sunday school teachers held at the Westhill Training College in Birmingham. The training lasted until December 18 and was made possible by the financing of the World Sunday School Association.

Pastor emeritus of The UMC in Estonia, Laas Helde, who comes from the village of Hänga, Sõrve peninsula in Saaremaa, can tell that under the leadership of Peeter Häng, the Torgu congregation displayed a great deal of Christian love and initiative toward the believers in the area. The village of Imara, about 25 km. (15 miles) from both the city of Kuressaare and the village of Torgu, needed a branch of the congregation started, as there were already some 20 believers in the village. On Ascension Day, May 18, 1939, Superintendent Martin Prikask and Pastor Peeter Häng placed a cornerstone for the Imara Prayer Chapel; and by December 10, 1939, they celebrated the consecration of the new building. The crowd that gathered as Superintendent Prikask lead the consecration service was too large to fit in the new building.

Although pastor Häng was mostly active in Torgu, he had a heart for evangelism and frequently visited various places in Estonia. This is evident from following the column in the *Kristlik Kaitsja (Christian Advocate)* magazine, entitled "Reports from the Homeland." Everywhere he preached the rooms were filled with both the young and the old. God was able to use Pastor Häng in a powerful way. As a result, many turned to God through hearing a message by Häng.

Peeter Häng also had a reputation among the people in his area, as did Pastor Karl Kuum, his predecessor. Laas Helde, whom Pastor Häng confirmed and accepted as a member into the Torgu congregation, confirms that Peeter Häng was, without exaggeration, called a holy man. He recalls once that when Pastor Häng entered a village store filled with rowdy men smoking and passing a bottle of vodka around, everyone fell silent. The bottles were tucked away, cigarettes put out, and even the elderly men took their pipes out of their mouths. After Pastor Häng left, people carried on as before, however, with not quite the same amount of enthusiasm.

Together with his wife, Peeter Häng did a great job at the spiritual education of the children. The attendance in Torgu Sunday School was between 50 and 80 children. In addition, there was the Junior's group, who were expected to have a bigger input into the life of the congregation than just any potential member.

Besides Karl Kuum and Peeter Häng, the Torgu congregation served as a springboard for such clergy as Konstantin Vipp, Aleksei Poobus, and Eduard Suurhans, all of whom were in full-time ministry.

The last words of Peeter Häng, uttered at the annual conference of the Estonian Methodist Church held in Tallinn's Petlemma congregation on February 24, 1940, were one of a prophet:

We are living at the spiritual midnight hour. We must be prepared and keep watch.

SUFFERING FOR THE SAKE OF CHRIST

The midnight hour came very swiftly for Peeter Häng. With the loss of Estonian independence in 1940, Peeter Häng lost his freedom. According to the information of the Kistler-Ritso Estonian Foundation, Peeter Häng of Torgu County, village of Hänga, was arrested along with his family by the Soviets in the first wave of deportations on July 1, 1941. Of the family only two members were spared: the eldest son George-Anatole, who was not at home at the time but visiting his grandmother Maria at the Hänga farm, and the third son, Leevi, who was critically ill and was left as it was assumed that he would die in any case. According to Lydia Häng they had been placed under arrest in the course of an emergency evacuation and were held in Harku prison in Tallinn, where the mother and five children were kept under arrest until September 17, 1941.[18] Peeter and Lydia lost all their valuables and money, such as watches, jewelry, souvenirs, items of gold or silver, including cash. All movable assets, such as furniture, books, and even clothing were seized, the doors of their house were sealed and locked. According to the KGB records, however, Peeter Häng was arrested on July 22, deported to Russia and kept under arrest in the city of Irkutsk.

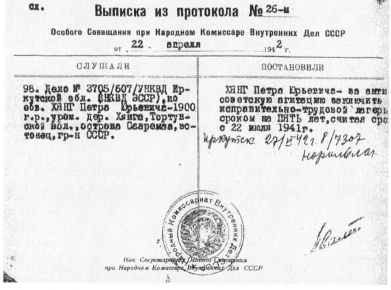

Abstract from the minutes of the extraordinary meeting of the People's Commissariat of Internal Affairs of the USSR, No. 26-m dated April 22, 1942.

[18]   As with the wives of Prikask and Prii, women and children were spared the trip to Siberia only because the unexpected Nazi invasion of the Soviet Union had caused chaos in the railway lines. See the chapter on Prikask for more details.

According to the documents, formerly kept in the KGB archives that became available after the fall of the Soviet Union, of the hearing dated December 31, 1941, Peeter Häng was accused of spreading anti-Soviet propaganda (in actuality it meant Christian work), preaching in the village of Hänga, distributing spiritual literature to the local believers, luring children to church by using material incentives such as presents, etc., and organizing religious education on Sundays. The case against him was passed on to the prosecutor's office, signed by the head investigator of the NKVD, Sergeant Agafonov and Senior Lieutenant Tihhomirov. Peeter Häng, as the accused, was forced to sign it. The document also bears the signature of the NKVD Junior Lieutenant Smirnov.

The next page contains the content of the case against him: working as a preacher of his religious beliefs. Peeter Häng was accused of making state-ments of anti-Soviet ideology thereby discrediting the Soviet authorities. Un- der the regulation of § 58–10 section 2, he was accused of distributing Christian literature, which he kept in the church, among the local population.

Based on verdict no. 001618 of the NKVD of the USSR from November 21, 1941, the case was to be heard at the extraordinary session of the People's Commissariat of Internal Affairs.

On February 16, 1942, in Irkutsk, based on overwhelming evidence of anti-Soviet and subversive activities toward the state in the case of Peeter Häng, son of Jüri, he was found guilty and sentenced to the highest punishment: execution by shooting and confiscation of all property.

However, an abstract of the minutes of the extraordinary meeting of the People's Commissariat of Internal Affairs of the USSR, No. 26-m dated April 22, 1942, shows that Peeter Häng was sentenced to five years in a forced labor camp, counting from July 22, 1941.

The last photograph of Peeter Häng, taken on January 8, 1942.

Much of Pastor Häng's tribulations suffered in Siberia were not documented and therefore can not be technically proven. Nevertheless, Leevi, son of Peeter Häng, met the General Secretary of the Estonian Communist Party, Vaino Väljas[19], in order to obtain more information concerning his father. He was granted access to the archives of the secret service and read the dossier of his father. According to his report, in addition to the sentence in the forced labor camp, Peeter Häng was sentenced to an additional five years of forced exile in Siberia. From there, his beloved father and the martyr of the Estonian Methodist Church never returned.

The exhausted body of Peeter Häng was utterly spent and not strong enough to cope with the extreme conditions of his incarcerations. He was called to his heavenly home on September 21, 1942, in Norillag, Krasnoyarsk *krai* of Russia. According to the prison medical records the cause of death was dysentery.

---

[19]   Vaino Väljas was the General Secretary of the Communist Party in Estonia between 1988 and 1990. (Translator's note)

Along with many others, Pastor Peeter Häng was officially rehabilitated as a victim of Stalinist repressions and declared innocent by the order No. 5/16, 1988, of the Supreme Court of the Soviet Socialist Republic of Estonia. As a result, the Fiscal Department of the Saare provincial government paid out to Leevi Häng as compensation a sum of 3,000 rubles.

Many precious memories of the enthusiastic preacher of the gospel remain along with plenty of good fruit from his ministry in the hearts of the believers in Saaremaa, a ministry for which Pastor Häng had to pay the highest price. Peeter Häng preferred "to be mistreated along with the people of God rather than to enjoy the pleasures of sin for a short time" (Hebrews 11:25). The fate of Häng's suffering in Siberia was also shared by Superintendent Martin Prikask of Kuressaare and Pastor Vassili Prii of Kõrkvere.

As for the fate of his family, the peninsula of Sõrve of the island of Saaremaa suffered great damage in the course of World War II. Most of the local villages were destroyed in the course of the war and the majority of the inhabitants were evacuated to Germany[20] by German troops. Peeter Häng's family was among them.

In the National Archives of Estonia, there is an entry containing Lydia Häng's biographical notes in which she writes that, when in the fall of 1944 German troops were retreating from the Sõrve peninsula, she along with her seven children was forcibly evacuated to Germany where she was moved from one camp to another. While in Germany, her daughter contracted an acute form of malaria that caused severe complications such as

---

[20] The forced evacuation of the local population from Sõrve peninsula (as well as from other regions of heavy fighting, such as the city of Narva and Ida-Virumaa region) was conducted by the German army in accordance with the Geneva Convention, which requires evacuation of local population from areas of active combat. Based on the available records, some 2,400 inhabitants of Sõrve peninsula were evacuated across the Baltic Sea to Germany from October 29 to 30, 1944, using ships that were taking supplies to the German troops stationed in Sõrve. (Translator's note)

arthritis and heart disease. After she was nursed back to health some eleven weeks later, they eventually were able to return to Estonia on October 7, 1945.

Due to heavy battles fought on the islands and on the western coast of Estonia, the losses suffered in the course of fighting were heavy. Likewise The Estonian Methodist Church bore heavy losses on the island of Saaremaa. The whole of the village of Imara was burned to the ground, including the newly consecrated Prayer Chapel. The Methodist church building in Torgu was also hit in the bombing.

Following the deportation of Pastor Häng on July 1, 1941, the work in the congregation was carried on by Pastor Eduard Raud, who continued serving the congregation until the imminent arrival of the Soviet army, at which time he and his wife evacuated to Sweden. After this, the congregation disintegrated and the people left, some to Germany, others to Sweden. Although the congregation suffered great loss, the vibrant faith kept alive in the hearts of the believers was taken with them wherever they went in the wide world, be it in the vast reaches of Siberia or across Europe.

Vassili Prii

(October 16, 1909 – September 30, 1942)

Who shall separate us from the love of Christ? Shall trouble or hardship or persecution or famine or nakedness or danger or sword?
Romans 8:35

Vassili Prii in the fall of 1935.

ENCOUNTER WITH THE LORD IN DECEMBER 1924

Katariina Prii was just a young girl when she left the island of Muhu to find employment on the mainland in one of the estates of the German nobility. Her service, however, was abruptly ended when she became pregnant by the son of the nobleman. This illegitimate son, born October 16, 1909, in the village of Suuremõisa, on the island of Muhu, was given the name Vassili and was to play an instrumental role in the history of The Methodist Church in Estonia.

Vassili's mother stayed on Muhu for only a brief period. Leaving her son in the care of relatives, she returned to mainland Estonia to pursue a frivolous, pleasure-filled lifestyle. Little is known of her later life, except that she mothered another child, a daughter Aino, with a man of Russian descent. At present there is no information concerning either the fate of Vassili's relatives or his half-sister Aino.

Vassili's adoptive family moved from Muhu to the neighboring island of Saaremaa. Upon completing the required elementary education, Vassili Prii earned his living putting up telephone poles in Orissaare, Saaremaa.

Vassili came to the Lord at age fifteen when Karl Kuum preached at a revival meeting in his childhood home in Saaremaa on December 14, 1924. The message preached by K. Kuum went straight to Vassili's heart, causing him to repent. After having asked Jesus into his heart and experiencing salvation, Vassili found peace and consolation for his heavy laden heart. At a youth meeting held over the Christmas holidays in 1924, at the request of pastor August Mikkov of the Pöide congregation, Vassili gave his first public testimony. It was uttered timidly at first, stuttering to find the appropriate words and with tears in his eyes. But he soon overcame the initial apprehension; and, as he later described the sensation,[21] he was overcome by the feeling that he had taken everybody in the audience up in his arms and carried them to the manger where Jesus lay and from there straight on to the foot of his cross. This first testimony given at Christmas was an impulse that encouraged him to dedicate his life to serving the Lord.

---

[21] Kristlik Kaitsja 1935, No. 12, p. 169.

God's Calling and the Lihula Congregation

God called Vassili to ministry quite early on, at barely eighteen years of age. At the semi-annual conference of the Baltic and Slavic Mission held in Riga, Latvia (January 26–28, 1927), Vassili Prii was appointed as lay preacher to Saaremaa.

Together with Alfred Tõns, his first missionary trip as a young preacher was to the island of Abruka in 1929, which proved to be an encouragement and a blessing. At the time the population of the island was around 130 people. In the previous year the island was visited by Martin Prikask, who had held a youth meeting there. As a result of preaching of the gospel by Brothers Prii and Tõns, God sent a spiritual revival among the islanders and seven married couples gave their lives to Christ. Eventually the number of believers on Abruka grew to include over thirty people, including twelve brothers actively involved in the ministry.

In 1929, at the historic Baltic Annual Conference[22] held in Tallinn (August 28–September 1), Bishop Wade appointed young Vassili Prii to lead the ministry in the Lihula congregation, situated in the western Estonian province of Läänemaa. In the town of Lihula, the Methodist congregation rented a spacious auditorium, where meetings were well attended, due to the active ministry of Vassili Prii and Ida Jõekalda. Vassili Prii's ministry in Lihula, however, was quite brief because in June of 1930, he was drafted into military service.

As a side remark, may it be noted, that the Lihula congregation is first mentioned in the annals of The Methodist Episcopal Church in 1923, when at the annual conference held in Riga, pastor Vilhelm Meinvald was appointed to lead the work there.

---

[22] In 1929, with over 25 ordained elders in the Baltic countries, the Baltic Annual Conference was formally organized.

Consecration of the Lihula congregational building in August, 1924. Vilhelm Meinvald is sitting in the front row, holding a child on his knee.

VILJANDI CONGREGATION

Viljandi[23] was officially named as the new field of ministry at the Baltic Annual Conference in 1929, with Philip Gildemann appointed as the leader to pioneer the ministry.

Two years prior, the Gildemann siblings, a brother and sister, had gathered many sympathizers to the Methodist work in the town of Viljandi. Mrs. Ormusson, a long-standing friend, had given the young congregation permission to meet in her house, which was located in the city center. Superintendent Prikask, while visiting Viljandi congregation, saw how people gathered at the meeting rooms three hours before the service started in order to ensure physically getting in.

---

[23] The city of Viljandi is the administrative center of Viljandimaa, in Southern Estonia located nearby the historic region of Mulgimaa, it was the home of Martin Prikask. (Translator's note)

At the 1931 Baltic Annual Conference held in Tallinn (August 5–9), young Vassili Prii, still doing his military service, was accepted as a probationary member of the annual conference.

Upon his release from the military the end of February 1932, Vassili returned for a short visit to his home on Saaremaa. As early as March 13 he traveled to Viljandi, following his appointment by the annual conference, to lead the work in Viljandi. At the Baltic Annual Conference held in Riga in 1932, Vassili Prii was ordained as a deacon and appointed to serve in Viljandi essentially in the capacity of local pastor.

By the time the congregation celebrated her third anniversary on March 8, 1933, they were renting the hall of the town cinema for worship services. In addition to the Viljandi congregation, Vassili Prii started the work of the Methodist youth association, the Epworth League, with 21 registered members. Prii described his ministry in Viljandi in the following modest words: *I manage, God be praised, not too badly. This is a hard place, but God has enough rain even for a place like Viljandi. We must pray more diligently!* [24]

Vassili Prii served the Viljandi congregation between 1932 and 1933, when he was replaced by Eduard Raud, a man who had been involved in full-time ministry since 1918.

MINISTRY IN THE TARTU II CONGREGATION

At the 1933 Baltic Annual Conference in Tallinn, Vassili Prii was accepted as a full member of the conference and appointed to serve as pastor in Tartu, replacing Pastor Jaan Jakobson (later Jaagupsoo). Pastor Prii, known for his warmth as well as for being a living witness of Christ, started his service in the Tartu II congregation on September 30, 1933.

---

[24] Kristlik Kaitsja (Christian Advocate), 1933, No. 1, p. 16.

Tartu II congregation was born on March 1, 1931, and stemmed from the local Blue Cross association. While serving in Tartu, Vassili Prii participated as a board member in the work of the humanitarian relief organization *Ühisabi*, which was lead by Aleksander Kuum. He also was on the board of the *Kodumisjon* (home mission) as treasurer, which was founded on March 19, 1934. The aim of the *Kodumisjon* was to send out evangelists, conduct charity work, and distribute Christian literature. Vassili Prii served in the Tartu II congregation as well as the Tartu Blue Cross for two years (1933–35). During that time he won over the Tartu parishioners and earned their affection with his kindheartedness and warm disposition.

MINISTRY IN THE PAIDE CONGREGATION

In 1935, at the extraordinary annual conference in Tallinn, during a festive ordination service held on a Sunday, with the ceremony of laying on hands, Bishop Raymond J. Wade, Superintendent Martin Prikask, and several senior brothers ordained Vassili Prii as an elder.

Vassili Prii was appointed as pastor to minister in the new congregation of Paide, replacing Eduard Raud, who had been the very first pastor in Paide, between 1934 and 1935.

The welcome service for Pastor Vassili Prii was held in Paide on October 6, 1935. Unfortunately he only served the local congregation less than a year before Bishop Raymond J. Wade appointed him as pastor to Pöide congregation on the island of Saaremaa.

Meanwhile, Paide congregation was troubled by a final eviction notice given by the owner of the meeting rooms. They had to move out in the summer of 1936, and it proved to be difficult to find new rooms. At a prayer evening people were turning to God in collective prayer for a building of their own. God does not turn down His children in their dire need.

Paide Methodist Congregation on the day of dedication in 1935. In the second row, left from the pulpit is seated Bishop Raymond J. Wade, on the right from the pulpit sits Superintendent Martin Prikask. Vassili Prii is standing in the back row, sixth from the left, behind the pulpit on the left.

Kõrkvere Church under construction in 1930. In the center row, fifth from the left is Vassili Prii, sixth is Alfred Tõns.

The answer was closer than expected: next door stood an industrial stone building, empty. It suited very well for a church building, given a few alterations. Negotiations with the local bank were started and came to an amicable arrangement: the building was acquired for a reasonable price, and on October 21, 1936, the deed was transferred to the church. Upon leaving the Paide congregation, Pastor Prii was replaced by Pastor Valdo Ojassoo.

PÖIDE CONGREGATION IN KÕRKVERE

The construction of the church building in Kõrkvere was started in 1930. Before winter set in, the walls and rafters were erected. The work was continued next spring and the consecration service was held already on Pentecost, while Alfred Tõns served as pastor. It is praiseworthy and should be noted that the local congregation was able to build the church with their own funds and without any additional debts. At the extraordinary annual meeting held in Tartu on July 29, 1936, Vassili Prii was appointed pastor in the Pöide congregation in Kõrkvere County, where he served between 1936 and 1941. Before his appointment, the former pastors who served there included: August Mikkov (1924–27) Martin Prikask (1926–28), Philip Gildemann (1928–29), Eduard Valdmann (1929–30), and Alfred Tõns (1930–1936).

The last place of appointment of Vassili Prii in Kõrkvere. In the center front row is Martin Prikask, on his right are seated Peeter Häng and Vassili Prii.

DEPORTATION FROM ESTONIA AND DEATH IN SIBERIA

At the Baltic Annual Conference in July of 1939, held in Tallinn, it was decided that Vassili Prii was to be sent to study in the Theological Seminary in Frankfurt, Germany. Unfortunately, it is not known whether he was able to pursue his education in theology in view of the complicated political situation in Europe. Vassili Prii attended the annual conference held in Tallinn's Petlemma congregation on Estonian Independence Day, February 24, 1940. The words he uttered on that day were: *Most important of all is that we would have love, as it is described by the apostle Paul in his First Epistle to the Corinthians chapter 13.*[25]

On March 22, 1941, Vassili married Marta Aer (October 13, 1914–August 13, 2001) of Pöide County, village of Ardla. They made their home in the village of Keskvere in Pöide County, where they lived in an apartment. Vassili and Marta were granted

---

[25]   Kristlik Kaitsja (Christian Advocate), 1940, No. 4, p. 59.

only a few months of marital happiness together during these difficult times and they did not have any children.

The last photograph of Vassili Prii.

His love and faith were tested in the course of the following persecutions. The first Soviet wave of mass deportation of Estonian people to Siberia tore Vassili and his wife Marta out of Saaremaa in July 1, 1941. On the way he was separated from his wife, and Marta was rerouted to Harku prison, where she spent one month.[26] Having returned to her home, she found it empty and gutted. Everything, down to the last piece of furniture as well as their clothes and other movable property, had been removed. (Most likely she was not expected to ever return.) Vassili was formally arrested on August 8, 1941, and was sentenced to three years in prison on April 15, 1942, based

---

[26] As with the wives of Prikask and Häng, women and children were spared the trip to Siberia only because the unexpected Nazi invasion of the Soviet Union had caused chaos in the railway lines. See the chapter on Prikask for more details.

on the verdict of the extraordinary meeting of the People's Commissariat of the Internal Affairs of the USSR.

His sentence was to be carried out in Norrilag, Irkutsk *oblast*, where he died on September 30, 1942.

Following the deportation of Vassili Prii, Kõrkvere congregation was pastored by Villem Õun, who served there from 1942 to 1945. The work was continued by Vassili's wife Marta Prii, between 1945 and 1948. Other ministers who have led the work there include: Jaan Puskay (1958–62), Aare-Jüri Ots (1962–65, 1997–2004), Eduard Lohv (1966–1985), Hjalmar Välisson (1985–1993), and Herni Kunstimees (1993–97).

The church in Kõrkvere has remained to this day as a monument to the days of blessing, reminding us of the men who have served their Lord. One such man was Pastor Vassili Prii, who gave his life for the sake of his witness of Christ.

Vassili Prii was declared to be an innocent victim of Stalinist repressions according to §1, section 2 of the act of "Rehabilitation of the Repressed persons convicted without a court hearing and wrongfully found guilty" passed by the Supreme Presidium of Estonian Soviet Socialist Republic on February 19, 1990. Following his official rehabilitation, the Fiscal Department of the Saaremaa provincial government paid out to his wife Marta compensation in the sum of 3,000 rubles on December 15, 1990. Naturally, this ridiculous amount of money would in no way compensate either his wife or Methodism in Estonia for the loss of Vassili Prii, along with many other people, men, women, and children, who were taken by force as victims of totalitarian power.

As of 2004, the Kõrkvere congregation is considered a branch of the Kuressaare congregation due to low membership. A few senior members of the congregation have transferred their membership to the Kuressaare Methodist Congregation.

Church can only function where there are people, and the population of the surrounding villages has dropped dramatically over the years. But even today, the beautiful surroundings and the church building in Kõrkvere serve as a pleasant place for arranging conferences and camps.

Hugo Oengo

(December 12, 1907 – December 10, 1978)

Remember your leaders, who spoke the word of God to you. Consider the outcome of their way of life and imitate their faith.
Hebrews 13:7

In this chapter I have used extracts from the writings of Hugo Oengo that date from 1960 and are found in the archives of the Church Board of The UMC in Estonia. These writings contain parts of an autobiography written on December 11, 1975, while Hugo Oengo served as superintendent. In addition I have made use of the memories of his daughter, Helgi Eenmaa. I am also grateful for access to Oengo family photographs as well as photographs by Eino Pärnamets. I have tried to combine these materials into one story in order to preserve the memory of Hugo Oengo for future generations.

Hugo Oengo was dedicated to serving the Lord. He gave up positions of honor in the secular world and an outstanding career for the sake of proclaiming the gospel of Christ under a totalitarian regime. He is an example of an exceptional hero of the cross. His uncompromising and self-sacrificing efforts for the glory of God were a true thorn in the flesh of militant Soviet atheists who tried to turn him into a public laughingstock by ridiculing him in the press. Nevertheless, God was able to use Hugo Oengo to save and heal many souls. His life holds for us all a valuable lesson.

Childhood

Hugo Oengo was born on December 12, 1907, in the city of Haapsalu. The eighth child in the family, he was given the name Hugo Arnold Öngo-Oengo. His father, Gustav, a sea captain of Swedish descent, had moved to the Estonian island of Hiiumaa. His grandfather on his father's side was also a sea captain and had a rented farm on the side. Since Hugo's father was away at sea for long periods of time, the weight of child-rearing was left on his mother's shoulders. His mother, Helene, came from a craftsman's family and was born on the island of Hiiumaa. She is described as a religious person, meek and balanced by nature. In Haapsalu the family lived in a cozy wooden townhouse. There were nine children in the family: seven boys and two girls; however, one of the boys, Artur (1902–1905) died at the age of three. Their father died in 1925, their mother in 1943. All the Oengo children are also in Glory now, Hugo having been the last to join them.

During Hugo's childhood years the family lived in a variety of places. Prior to his birth, up until 1904, their home was on the island of Hiiumaa, at which time they moved to the city of Haapsalu on the mainland. In 1913, they moved to the capital city of Tallinn, and then, in 1918, the family returned to Haapsalu.

Hugo's special connection to Haapsalu Methodist Congregation goes back to his early years when he attended their Sunday school and children's services.

Family portrait from 1914. Standing besides his father, in the front row, first from the right is Hugo Oengo.

Hugo Oengo came to Christ at the age of 17. Prior to that he experienced unrest in his soul and felt his life had no purpose. He recorded for us his prayer, "Lord, You can send peace in my heart. If this is Your desire then please answer me!" The next day there was an answer. An old friend, whom he had not seen for a long time, had become a believer. When he came to visit Hugo, the latter was engaged in a card game with his schoolmates. Let us just say that this particular game of cards was never finished. As a result of the conversation with his visiting friend, Hugo gave his life to Jesus while still sitting at that card table. His heart was filled with peace. Following his conversion he witnessed at school, telling his friends about Jesus, a witness he continued to bear until the very end of his days. In 1924, he became a member of Haapsalu

Methodist Episcopal Congregation as well as the Methodist youth society, the Epworth League.

STUDENT YEARS

Hugo Oengo's primary education began in Tallinn and continued in the city of Haapsalu, where he finished Haapsalu Secondary School *cum laude* in 1926. In the same year he enrolled in the Tallinn College of Engineering (today called the Tallinn University of Technology) where he began his studies in civil engineering. Due to the family's financial situation, Hugo Oengo supported his studies by working at various summer jobs. Between 1924 and 1926, he was employed surveying harbors and as an engineering supervisory technician with various construction projects. In 1927, he worked at the construction of Mõisaküla railroad and, in 1928, at the department of road construction in the northeastern region of Estonia called Virumaa.

Selma and Hugo Oengo.

Despite the financial support offered toward his education by his brother and sister, his funds were insufficient to fully cover his studies. So, in the fall of 1928, he started as a junior lab assistant. The laboratory was led by Professor Ottomar Maddison and investigated the technical properties of construction materials and metals, participating in the work of the State Laboratory of Materials Testing and was involved in the publishing of volume 3 of *Technical Mechanics.* Later Oengo was involved in teaching technical mechanics and structural engineering.

Hugo Oengo graduated with a degree in civil engineering, with a fairly wide area of specialization: bridges, roads, and hydromechanics. Having performed his required practice, he received his full license on September 29, 1934, and was accepted as a full member of the Chamber of Engineers. A most productive cooperation with the outstanding Estonian professor of civil engineering, Ottomar Maddison, lasted some 22 years, until March 1950. Under Ottomar Maddison's tutelage, Hugo Oengo drew up several engineering projects for bridges as well as expert evaluations on civil engineering projects.

The first Board of the Epworth League Alliance in 1927. In the center of the first row is Dr. George A. Simons. First from the right seated, is the first Chairman of the Board, composer Johan Tamverk. Back row: second from the right, Hugo Oengo.

In 1933, Hugo Oengo married Selma Uuetoa, sister to his friend Harri Uuetoa. Their wedding took place in Tallinn on the eve of Pentecost in the Methodist church on Veerenni Street. By 1934, Hugo Oengo was already active as a lay preacher in the Tallinn Methodist Congregation, chairman of the Epworth League, as well as board member of the Youth Association of The Methodist Episcopal Church in Estonia. From August 2 to 5, 1934, Hugo Oengo represented Estonia as a delegate at the Finnish Methodist Youth Conference. The Finnish hosts characterized him as a dedicated, god-fearing, educated young man, and published a couple of his speeches along with his photo in the Finnish Methodist magazine, *Rauhan Sanomia*.

TARTU PERIOD 1934–1936

In 1934, Hugo Oengo was transferred to the University of Tartu where a faculty of technology was founded. He worked there as a senior assistant, as well as an assistant instructor, teaching structural mechanics and bridges until the summer of 1936. That summer he worked part-time for a Danish company, Hoigard and Schultz in the city of Pärnu where he participated as an engineer in the construction of the municipal bridges of Suursild, Siimu, Tori, and Pikasilla.

By appointment of the extraordinary annual conference, which took place in Tallinn, September 7–10, 1935, Hugo Oengo was appointed as pastor in the city of Tartu where he took over the reins from Vassili Prii who in turn was transferred to the Paide congregation. At the same time he was elected a member of the church board to work side-by-side as one of the closest co-workers of Martin Prikask, along with Ferdinand Tombo, Adalgoth Seck, Aleksander Kuum, and Harri Uuetoa.

Even before the Soviet occupation, during his professional career in Tartu, Oengo experienced disdain and discrimination for his religious beliefs. Non-Lutheran Christians were generally shunned, regardless of the fact that the University of Tartu had a faculty of theology and the rector of the university, Dr. Johannes Kõpp, was himself a professor of theology. Oengo applied time and time again for a grant to further his studies abroad, however, without any success. The reasons for refusing him a scholarship were not commented on in any way. Later he heard from one of the leading figures in the decision-making process, that the reason was simply his involvement in "a religious sect." Receiving such a grant as well as any further teaching positions in the university was made dependent upon his leaving The Methodist Church.

However, as Oengo himself used to say, those who put their hope in God will not be ashamed. In the summer of 1936, the faculty of technology in Tartu was closed and Hugo Oengo was transferred back to Tallinn to the newly opened Technical Institute,[27] where he worked as an assistant instructor, at the same time as he continued his own studies. In January of 1937, he received his postgraduate degree *cum laude* in the field of civil and building engineering.

ON SCHOLARSHIP TO SWITZERLAND

From October 1937 until March 1939, Hugo Oengo, accompanied by his wife Selma, lived in Switzerland on a scholarship granted jointly by the Tallinn Technical University and the Ministry of Economic Affairs. Oengo continued his doctoral studies at the University of Zürich as well as at the Swiss Federal Institute of Technology under the supervision of the world-renowned professor Mirco Gottfried Rosh. Oengo participated in the work group researching several major bridges and construction projects, which are noted in the published scientific works of Professor

---

[27] By the September 15, 1936, Act of the Head of State, the former Tallinn College of Engineering was granted the status of University, named Tallinn Technical Institute. In 1938, the name was officially changed to Tallinn Technical University. (Translator's note)

Rosh. In Zürich, Oengo wrote a doctoral dissertation on the theory of reinforced concrete. Unfortunately he was unable to defend this dissertation due to the outbreak of World War II. However, Oengo was very determined; and between 1944 and 1946 he wrote a new doctoral dissertation on the topic of the theory of plates. He defended his dissertation in 1946 in the Tallinn Polytechnic Institute (as the university was called during Soviet time) and received a Ph.D. in civil engineering.

Hugo and Selma in Zürich.

In April 1939, Hugo returned from Switzerland to Tallinn, Estonia, and was hired as an expert engineer and senior assistant in Tallinn Technical University (renamed Tallinn Polytechnic Institute in 1941). In the autumn of the same year he was elected as adjunct professor for reinforced concrete constructions. The decision of the university was confirmed by the Act of the Head of State in January 1940. Oengo was able to work in his new position until he was forcibly mobilized into the Red Army in 1941.

INTENSE PROFESSIONAL YEARS IN TALLINN AND SUBSEQUENT MOBILIZATION

Until his mobilization into the Soviet Army on July 27, 1941, Hugo Oengo led a very intense scientific and academic life. He was jointly supervising the engineering and construction phases of the Maardu phosphorous plant (September 1940 to July 1941) and was lecturing at the Tallinn Technical University (January 1940 to July 1941). In addition he was often invited to consult on matters of civil and building engineering. He was also hired part-time as an on-staff expert by the city of Tallinn's Soviet municipal government (September 1940 to July 1941). It is during this period that Oengo started his in-depth research on the use of burnt shale as a binder in construction technology. As a result of his research a factory was built to realize his discovery.

In addition to all this professional work, he was continuing to bear the pastor's responsibilities in the second Tallinn Methodist congregation, known as the Sitsi or Petlemma Prayer Chapel. In other words, he bore the responsibilities of many men.

The Soviet annexation of Estonia and the onset of World War II brought conscription into the Red Army. Oengo had an inner conviction that he was not to try to escape the draft or ask for an extension but was to accept it and go. Later, Nigol Andresen, a People's Commissary in charge of education, told Oengo that he did not really need to go with the draft since he could have probably received an extension. Looking back, we can see God's leading. Others, who were granted an extension, remained in Estonia when German occupation temporarily pushed out the Soviets. Many of these people later escaped to the West before the Soviets returned on the heels of the retreating German army. In choosing to flee to safety they ended up being separated from their people and their country for a very long time. Oengo, on the other hand, by going with the Soviet draft, ended up staying in his native country to do God's work among his people.

Hugo Oengo himself was far away from his native land and his loved ones, but only from July 27, 1941, until October 9, 1944. On July 27, 1941, he closed his apartment door behind him utterly convinced that his hand would not be opening it again. Mobilization had begun into the Red Army construction battalions located in Siberia. What followed were illness, cold, and hunger, altogether eight long months of service as a private in the Estonian Construction Battalion of the Red Army in the village of Rezh of Sverdlovsk administrative district. God was truly with him in all these difficult circumstances. He survived, when, due to incredible hardship and poor living conditions nearly one-third of all conscripts perished during the winter months of 1941/42.

On March 26, 1942, Oengo was assigned to the reserve of experts operating under the Council of People's Commissars of the Estonian Soviet Socialist Republic. In April 1942, he was stationed in the city of Sverdlovsk (present day Yekaterinburg) east of the Ural Mountains, in the Ural Industrial Institute named after S. M. Kirov where he worked until September 17, 1944. At first Oengo acted as senior consultant in the consultation bureau working out of the institute, and during the academic year of 1943/44 as the assistant professor in the strength of materials and structural mechanics department. It is during this time that the highest Soviet attestation committee accredited him with an academic title of *docent*, according to the regulations of the USSR. As his former degree was attested by the president of Estonian Republic, it was not acceptable in the Soviet Union.

In Sverdlovsk, as professor, he failed a student who happened to be the local communist youth secretary. The student went to complain about his teacher, claiming that the "fascist," as people from the Baltic countries were commonly branded, had intentionally failed him because he was the leader of the local branch of the communist youth organization, *Komsomol*. A repeat examination was arranged before a commission of experts, however, and the student again failed. Oengo, in his statement to the expert review commission, said that one cannot expect him to make an exception and pass a student simply because he is a *Komsomol* secretary. This person by his position is expected all the more to be a true example of fine scholarship. He went on to explain to the commission that, "I could not afford to have my students learn their specialty so poorly that the bridges they engineer will collapse." The leadership of the university, no doubt, had to agree with Oengo.

Oengo was allowed to return to Estonia on October 9, 1944. He picked up right where he had left off, continuing his work in the church. By this time, however, the first Tallinn church had been destroyed in the Soviet bombing raid of March 9, 1944, which had devastated the city's residential districts, leaving some 20,000 people homeless in a single night. With the loss of the large Veereni Street church building, the members of Tallinn's first and second congregations were now part of a joint Methodist congregation under the leadership of Aleksander Kuum. Oengo began teaching in the Tallinn Polytechnic Institute, a professional career that became increasingly demanding. In July 1948, Oengo was required, in addition to his academic and research work at the institute, to participate in the work of state construction companies.

Over the years, Oengo organized the scientific research department at the institute and led its activity for several years. He was also a member of the Scientific Advisory Board of the Tallinn Polytechnic Institute as well as a member of its committee for evaluating entrance examinations. He was a permanent member of the expert committee of the State Planning Commission as well as a member of the council of technology of the Ministry of

Construction. From February 1947, Oengo worked as division head in the Institute of Architecture and Construction of the newly founded Academy of Science of the Estonian Soviet Socialist Republic. Last but not least, he was a member of the Council of Technical Engineering Unions and a member of the board of the state civil engineering department.

A joyous event of a personal nature took place in the spring of 1946, with an addition to the Oengo family. A daughter, Helgi, was adopted, with whom the happy parents were able to share abundant parental love. Up to this point Hugo and Selma had lived in the parsonage of the second Tallinn congregation. But in the summer of 1948, with a growing family, Hugo Oengo undertook a construction project of his own. In addition to his professional career, he started building a home for his family. Given the difficult economic circumstances at

Selma and Hugo with their daughter Helgi in 1949, standing in front of their apartment located in the Petlemma Prayer Chapel at No. 92A, Kopli Street.

the time, it was a very challenging task. However, a decent salary combined with clever economizing wherever possible, allowed him to complete the house by March of 1950. Oengo used to tell how there was a special blessing over their house project, so that even the state loan bonds and obligations he had invested in miraculously started producing, one after another.

SCIENTIFIC AND OTHER LITERATURE

From the central electronic database of Estonian libraries one can find nine entries under the name Hugo Oengo, dating between 1937 and 1949. As a recognized specialist on construction materials, his name appears in connection with seven books, which he authored or co-authored. Of these, two were published in foreign languages.

On the Prediction of the 28-day Compressive Strength of Concrete Mixtures using Estonian Portland-cement. O. Maddison and H. Oengo. Tallinn, 1938.

Die statische Tragfähigkeit der auf Biegung und exzentrischen Druck beanspruchten Eisenbetonkörper. H. Oengo. Tartu: Teaduslik Kirjandus, 1941.

In addition to scientific literature, two other articles have been published of a religious nature, one being the speech he delivered at the tenth Evangelical Alliance Conference in Tallinn on May 18, 1937, and the other contains an article in the collection of writings *Ülim Soov (The Utmost Desire)*, which he wrote while in Zürich in June of 1938. In his youth he wrote some fine religious poems which were published in the *Kristlik Kaitsja (Christian Advocate)* magazine.

YEARS OF RELIGIOUS PERSECUTION

In 1947, a campaign of anti-religious propaganda in the Soviet Union was launched. As a result, Hugo Oengo ended up under surveillance in his professional career both at the Polytechnic Institute as well as at the Academy of Science. The overall results of the investigation were quite positive, considering the legal requirements of the time. The only shortcoming was considered to be his religious piety and preaching in the church. In October 1947, Oengo was summoned to meet with Comrade Kuzmin, the Secretary of Personnel of the Central Committee of the Estonian

Communist Party. The discussion revolved around Oengo's religious activity, which, according to the Soviet functionary, was not befitting his position in the university. Oengo, on the other hand, pointed out to his opponent that the constitution of the USSR guarantees freedom of conscience, the right to profess any religion and to conduct religious worship. He added that there are no legal restrictions limiting this freedom for people in professional positions. The secretary of the Central Committee still strongly suggested that Oengo stop his religious activities, advice Oengo rejected.

In July 1948, Oengo was dismissed from his position as lecturer of the Polytechnic Institute by order of the Minister of Higher Education of the USSR. The reason for his firing was recorded simply with the word "inappropriate." However, Oengo's own employment record book shows four excellent entries in addition to being awarded a Medal for Meritorious Labor. During the Great Patriotic War. The fact is, he was branded as unsuitable solely for being a Christian and working in a religious organization that, ironically, was actually permitted by Soviet law.

Following his dismissal, Oengo took up a full-time position in the Academy of Science, where he had previously worked on a part-time basis. But relentless religious discrimination soon caught up with him there. It was not long before it was clear that there was a predisposition to find fault with his work. The division placed under his leadership was, however, one of the most successful, keeping pace with the demands of the day through its relevant topics of research. Nevertheless, Hugo Oengo was dismissed in March of 1950, after he refused to give in his notice "on his own initiative."

Being hired as a senior engineer in the civil engineering bureau of the Ministry of Communal Affairs in the summer of 1950 came as a surprise to Oengo. He was able to work in this position until the fall of 1955. Being a sought-after specialist, he was able to work part-time as a head constructor in the Tallinn division of the Paper and Cellulose Industry State Engineering Institute as well as in the Tallinn Shipbuilding Company supervising the project of restoring the ship-lifting mechanism as constructor-in-chief.

BLESSED YEARS IN THE CHURCH AT MERE PUIESTEE

After the large Methodist church building on Veerenni Street was destroyed during the Soviet bombing raid of March 9, 1944, the two Tallinn Methodist congregations merged into one, using the Petlemma Prayer Chapel in the Kopli region of the city. This sanctuary, specifically built by The Methodist Church, had been home to the second Tallinn Methodist congregation since being dedicated in January, 1935. Sadly, this building was not destined to remain as a church; and on July 9, 1950, the final service took place in a Methodist-owned church building in Tallinn. A few days later the church building was commandeered by the Soviet Army for use as a military radio station.[28]

Despite being made homeless, many blessed years of spiritual work followed in the church at No. 3 Mere Puiestee. The church building, which provided shelter to the homeless Methodist congregation, actually belonged to the Seventh Day Adventists; and permission to use it for Methodist services had to be granted by Commissioner Kivi of the Council of Religious Affairs of the USSR's Council of Ministers. Permission was granted for a three-month period. This permit, dated July 16, 1950, grew into a 50-year cohabitation of the two congregations,

---

[28] In 1991, just months before Estonia regained independence, the old Petlemma Prayer Chapel would be demolished by the Soviet authorities. Nine years later, in September 2000, Tallinn Methodists would dedicate the newly completed sanctuary in the Baltic Mission Center, ending 50 years of homelessness. (Translator's note)

which resulted in seven worship services being held each week under one roof in peace and mutual understanding.

The church at No. 3, Mere Puiestee.

When Aleksander Kuum, the senior pastor of the Tallinn congregation was sentenced to 25 years in a Siberian prison camp in May of 1952, Hugo Oengo stepped in as senior pastor. At the end of 1955, Oengo gave up his professional career and dedicated himself full time to pastoral ministry. Upon Aleksander Kuum's fortunate return from Siberia in July 1956 after only four years in the prison camp, the partnership of the two men in steering the congregation continued where it had left off.

Services in the church at Mere Puies-tee were always well attended as God sent a spiritual revival in the early 1950's and the congregation grew. Every Tuesday and Thursday evening two services were held, one at five and one at seven o'clock, in order to meet the growing numbers. At the end of the each meeting, Hugo Oengo had to kindly request his five o'clock crowd to vacate the church hall to make room for the people coming for the next

service. Three services would be held on Sundays: at 10:00, at
12:30 (in Russian language), and again at 3:30. Christians from
other denominations often visited Methodist services on a regular
basis as the Holy Spirit was moving powerfully in The Methodist
Church. There were instances when, in response to the altar call,
there were dozens of people coming to the front in repentance
to give their lives to God. On many occasions God used Brother
Oengo powerfully to heal the sick in response to his prayers. Still
today there are people who can witness to having been restored to
health in miraculous ways through Oengo's ministry. The former
senior pastor of Tallinn's St. Olav's Baptist Church, Rein Uuemõis,
once said, looking back at this time, that the church at Mere
Puiestee became popular among believers as the place where
God was at work. Estonian Christians used to recommend to
alcoholics, "If you wish to be free, go to Mere Puiestee Church."

Rebuilding work in 1958 at Methodist headquarters located at No. 3, Apteegi Street.

Hugo Oengo and Paul Kornel supervised the construction
project, and under their management the work went smoothly.

On May 4, 1958, the work began by hauling away the rubble. One year later, on May 5, 1959, the first board meeting was held in the new facility; and in January of 1960, upon passing the required inspection, the building was officially approved for use. The work was completed by the hard work of church members, from the old to the young. Even I remember how, as a young boy, I helped along with other believers to nail the plasterboard to the walls.

Selma and Hugo on their 25th wedding anniversary in 1958.

In 1958, Hugo and Selma Oengo celebrated their 25th wedding anniversary. Hugo had a very good sense of humor and he made contact very easily with other people. According to their daughter, Helgi, they lived as a very close family. She once wrote, "My dad was good at every kind of handiwork, whether fixing shoes or building a tile stove or making a wood carving. However, it had to be urgent before he would get around to it. He had plenty of writing to do, so that at times he worked nights on end. In everything he did, he was very diligent and demanding in regards to himself first and also others. When there were rare disagreements between the couple, Selma always knew how to disperse all tension with her feminine wisdom."

In November 1966, Hugo Oengo was made another professional offer that he accepted alongside working as pastor, and this last period of his engineering career lasted until January 1, 1975. During this time he worked from November 1966 to May 1974 in the "EKE Projekt," a state engineering company engaged in rural construction projects for the collective farms. His second place of employment was as laboratory and division head in the State Agro-Industrial Committee's Scientific Manufacturing enterprise from May 1974 to January1975. One of the most prominent projects from this period was the project of the EKE Palivere construction materials factory, where Oengo was head engineer and responsible for the civil engineering plans. Even after retiring, Oengo continued as consultant for the same state company. Over this period he attended Soviet-wide and international scientific symposiums in Frunze (1969), Berlin (1971) where he delivered a speech, Irkutsk (1973), and Tallinn (1975).

Sadly, it was also during this same period that Hugo's beloved wife Selma died on June 4, 1973. She was laid to rest at Tallinn's Rahumäe Cemetery, ending a marriage that had lasted forty blissful years.

SUPERINTENDENT OF THE METHODIST CHURCH IN ESTONIA

At the annual conference of The United Methodist Church in Estonia in 1974, Hugo Oengo was elected superintendent. In addition to his new position, he also continued serving as pastor of the Tallinn congregation alongside Olav Pärnamets, who was appointed there from Paide in June 1970 to take over Kuum's position as pastor. Kuum served as superintendent between 1962 and 1974, and again between 1978 and 1979.

God did not let Hugo Oengo remain a widower for long. On June 17, 1975, he married Liis Ploom, a member of the Tallinn Methodist congregation. The wedding ceremony was conducted by Superintendent Emeritus Aleksander Kuum.

Hugo Oengo's first official visit in the capacity of superintendent was to participate, together with Aleksander Kuum, in the meeting held in Moscow, on September 29, 1975, under the leadership of Patriarch Pimen of the Russian Orthodox Church. The purpose of the meeting was to discuss preparations for the Conference of Interdenominational Pro-peace Church Clerics, which would be held in Moscow, July 1–10, 1977.

In 1976, Oengo was able to twice travel outside the Soviet Union, a very rare event in those days. He visited East Germany and the city of Karl-Marx-Stadt to attend their Methodist Central Conference and in November

The wedding ceremony of Liis and Hugo Oengo in 1975, celebrated in the church on Mere Puiestee.

Hugo Oengo speaking in the Lutheran Church of the Holy Ghost in Tallinn, at the service dedicated to the 70th anniversary of the Estonian Methodist Church in 1977.

he traveled to Stavanger, Norway, to the Central Conference of The United Methodist Church in Northern Europe. On the way home from Norway he also spent a few days in Sweden.

In May of 1976, Oengo was invited to participate in The UMC's General Conference in Portland, Oregon. However, this remained merely an invitation, since the Soviet officials did not grant him permission to leave the country. Regardless, Oengo was elected as member of the Executive Committee of the World Methodist Council and in the fall of 1978 he was able to take part in the committee's meeting in London at the time Wesley's Chapel was re-opened. During the same visit he had the honor to meet Queen Elizabeth II.

Hugo Oengo participated as one of the main speakers at the annual conference of The United Methodist Church in Finland held at Vesivehmaa (August 3–7, 1977), where he preached on the topic "A Living Congregation." Following the conference he visited nearly every Methodist congregation in Finland.

Hugo Oengo had the privilege to celebrate his 70th birthday in the same year The Methodist church also turned 70. The celebrations were postponed from June until October 7–10, 1977. The festive closing ceremony was held in the Lutheran Church of the Holy Ghost in Tallinn. The guest list included Dr. Joe Hale, Secretary General of the World Methodist Council; Bishop Ole E. Borgen; Dr. Vello Salo from Canada; Bishop Finis A. Crutchfield Jr.; Finnish Superintendent Pentti Järvinen; and many others.

On that festive day no one could imagine that already the very next year on December 10, 1978, the Lord would call His servant to join Him in glory, away from this land of struggle. Only a year earlier, Oengo had said to his sisters and brothers in Finland, "We do not have a paved highway before us, but on this road we are on the side of the Victorious One. Therefore our toil in the Lord is not in vain."

His funeral was worthy of a statesman. The memorial service was held at St. Olav's Church in Tallinn on December 16, 1978. He is buried at Tallinn's Rahumäe Cemetery beside his beloved first wife Selma.

Indeed, regarding Brother Hugo Oengo, God's Word is true, *"Blessed are the dead who die in the Lord from now on." "Yes," says the Spirit, "they will rest from their labor, for their deeds will follow them."* (Revelation 14:13)

Funeral of Hugo Oengo. From left to right: Liis Oengo, Superintendent Emeritus Aleksander Kuum, Superintendent Olav Pärnamets, Ralf Uusmäe. From right to left: members of the Church Board, Toomas Pajusoo and Raivo Kõrgemägi, placing a wreath on the grave of Hugo Oengo.

Aleksander Kuum
(SEPTEMBER 21, 1899 – FEBRUARY 12, 1989)

PAGES FROM MY LIFE'S BOOK[29]

Aleksander Kuum.

And I saw the dead, great and small, standing before the throne, and books were opened. Another book was opened, which is the book of life. The dead were judged according to what they had done as recorded in the books. Revelation 20:12

The books were opened, great and small were standing before the throne. In these words the prophet describes the Last Judgment: a verdict made "according to what was recorded in the books."

I will make a humble attempt at recording a few pages of my life's book. I am well aware that it is seen through human eyes and human judgments. Oh Lord, be merciful when you measure my life with your measuring stick!

---

[29] An autobiographical account, written in Tallinn, 17 March 1959 at 5.45 AM.

EARLY CHILDHOOD

I was born September 21, 1899. My father, Karl,[30] was at the time a tenant farmer, farming land that belonged to others, in the northeastern region of Virumaa, near the village of Pala in Vohnja County. My mother, Liisa (maiden name Brock), was a distiller's daughter from the Udriku estate. Both were Estonian by nationality.

Aleksander Kuum's parents, Karl and Liisa.

Our home was situated in the marshlands nearly 20 kilometers from the city of Tapa toward the coast. We left there when I was six, but I still recall the sandpit behind the house, the stream in the pasture, the choke cherry trees, and the meadow by the river Valgejõe. Oh, how I have loved since early childhood the nature of my homeland, her modest beauty!

On December 26, 1902, my father received assurance of his salvation. This jolly and jovial man had sometime earlier been touched by God in a wonderful way. Now he became a living witness to Christ who led many to the Lord through preaching at evangelistic meetings. In 1905, we took up residence in the city of Tapa. When Methodism came to Estonia, he joined the Methodists and built a small prayer chapel by our house. From

---

[30] Karl Kuum (1867–1933) was one of the very first Estonian Methodist pastors. Together with Vassili Täht, he preached in the evangelistic meetings on Saaremaa in June of 1907 which launched Methodism in Estonia and saw Martin Prikask commit his life to Christ. Karl Kuum was born in northeastern Estonia, in Vohnja County. Active as an evangelist in Estonia and Russia, he became a Methodist elder in the city of Tapa (1912), church planter in the city of Pärnu (1921) and in Torgu County (1924). He continued to pastor in Torgu, Saaremaa, up until his death.

Tapa he traveled near and far, all across Estonia and into the regions of the Russian Empire.

THE TRIALS OF WORLD WAR I

I started school in Tapa Elementary School and later studied at Tapa Secondary School, which I graduated from in 1914, at the onset of World War I. Taking the advice I was given, I did not go on to study in the university but instead, to avoid ending up on the battlefield as a conscript, I applied for work on the railroad, in the Tapa office. However, the war rolled on and eventually reached the city of Tapa. I remember a foggy morning in April when the German troops arrived in the Tapa station by train, soldiers with machine guns sitting on a platform car, pushed by the locomotive in the front of the train. German occupation had begun: a gloomy "bans and commands" era. It was as if life froze. There was no work. My young heart longed for happiness and adventure.

Thus one day I stood before my parents and said, "I am going to Russia." The slogan "Liberty, Equality, Fraternity" was very alluring. My mother broke out in tears. I was her only son and the baby of the family; my two sisters were older than I. Father, however, said, "If he does not like it at home, let him go and look for his happiness elsewhere."

Thus one day I stood before my parents and said, "I am going to Russia." In Petrograd[31] I was reinstated on the railway, even paid for the time I had missed out and stationed as a clerk in the city of Jamburg.[32] Did it ever feel great in the beginning! I could come and go as I pleased. Neither mother's tears nor father's

---

[31] St. Petersburg, Russia, was renamed Petrograd after the communist revolution. After the death of Lenin it was again renamed, Leningrad.
[32] Present day, Kingissepp. Located in Russia, 120 km (75 miles) southwest of St. Petersburg and 20 km (12 miles) east of the Estonian city of Narva.

admonitions could cloud my happiness. And being young and healthy, there was lots of fun and entertainment to be found at first.

Yet, my life story also resembles the one of the prodigal son. While I was abroad, like in the story, *there was a severe famine in that whole country*. I was walking on the high banks of the Luga River and thinking, "If I could only find a loaf of bread – as big and round and sweet-smelling as the ones my mother bakes!" There was no bread, but one had to find sustenance. We ate cakes made out of potato skins and horse meat. I am reminded of a scene I witnessed while riding a streetcar on one of the main streets of Petrograd. A cabby's horse collapsed of hunger in the middle of the street. At once a crowd gathered around the horse and carriage. When I passed by the same spot on my way back, there was nothing but a skeleton of the horse left on the street. An old lady was trying hard to break the horse's head off the backbone. It could be boiled into headcheese!

Meanwhile I was stationed at Gattshina, some 45 kilometers (28 miles) south of Petrograd. Russia was now caught up in civil war in every region and that, in turn, cut off my chances of getting back home to Estonia. Now I was constantly thinking about my father's house, where there was plenty of food. But major tribulations were still to come.

In 1919, I was mobilized to the Red Army and sent to the Polish front. Here, amidst the atrocities of war, I thought to myself, "I would eat plain bread and sardines and sleep under the spruce tree, if only I did not have to kill people and let others try to kill me!" War is a terrible thing! One day there was particularly fierce fighting going on. My friends were being slain left, right, and center. The fire from the machine guns was so heavily upon us that in the alder grove where we were getting ready to charge, it felt like we were caught in an autumn storm with all the leaves and branches falling on us cut down by the bullets. I remember praying for the first time in a long while. I said, "God, I am not worthy to be heard by You. But for the sake of my parents' prayers please save me from this hell and I promise to give my life to You!"

RETURN OF THE PRODIGAL SON

God delivered me. I was wounded, and when I was released from hospital there was an opportunity to opt to go home, to Estonia. So it was that one fine day I stood before my parents again filled with joy. The son *that was dead was alive again.*

However, that joy was only temporary. I was alive, but as far as I was concerned, God was dead. I broke my promise to God and indulged in the pleasures of sin. Having left home a skeptic, I had now started to deny the existence of God and had to find ways to mollify my conscience to escape the fear of death and judgment. One morning, having returned from a party, my father's expression was more stern than usual. He said, "Your mother and I have not slept this night. We were praying for you. We prayed like it says in the Bible, 'God, better let our son lose an eye, hand, or leg. It is better for him to go to heaven as a cripple than go to hell a whole man.' " This was very painful for me to hear, and now, as a parent, I understand how difficult it must have been for my parents. Then followed a time when I felt like King David, "For day and night your hand was heavy upon me" (Psalm 32:4). I was unemployed, tailed by both the police and the spiritual revival that was happening among the young people in the city of Pärnu where my parents were serving at the time. The end result of all of this had a wonderful effect on me, and the spiritual breakthrough in my life was not far behind.

However, it was not until 1921, two days after Christmas that the breakthrough arrived. At my parents' request I had taught some new converts a few Christmas carols, which they sang at a youth meeting. How zealously they performed them and gave their testimonies! Again new people came to the front of the church to give their life to Jesus. Everybody was praising God overwhelmingly. However, when everybody had left, I stood alone in the middle of the sanctuary feeling as if I had missed the train. It was as if everybody had gone to a big joyful celebration and I was not included. I pressed my burning hot forehead against a window pane and looked out. It was snowing outside – big flakes were softly coming down. Everything was white, but there was a raging storm in my heart. My heart was black. I fought to hold back tears.

My father found me and told me to go to bed. My bed was across the room from my parents'. My father must have noticed something, because all of a sudden he said, "Son, God is calling you tonight! Give your heart over to Him!" I could not utter a word; it was as if my lips were clamped shut. My father started to explain to me the Scriptures, speaking as if he knew all the doubts in my soul. He asked again, "Son, would you like to pray with me?" I did want to pray, but I could not utter a word. Then my mother joined in, suggesting that we talk in the morning. But I thought to myself, "If you only knew what is at stake right now you would not speak this way! Should Dad ask again, I will answer right away!" And so he did. In response I said, no I shouted, "Yes, let's pray!" When the three of us: me, my mom and dad, were kneeling in the dark room, I prayed along with my parents. I said, "God, if you exist, please reveal yourself to me. And if you forgive my sins and grant peace in my heart, I promise to give my life to You as of this hour." This was on December 27, 1921 at 5A.M.

That morning I felt wonderful peace in my heart. Christ had won. The doubts were gone. Satan did test my willpower in many different ways, be it through a lucrative job offer, or temptation; but, praise the Lord, this very night over Christmas holidays was the turning point in my life.

After having been pardoned for my sins and found the assurance of salvation, my Maker promptly called me to tend to His vineyard. Thus it was that on the fourth day after my salvation I found myself standing in the pulpit. It was New Year's Eve 1921. Pärnu Methodist Church was full to the brim. My knees were shaking and my voice was trembling when I read from Revelation 7:14 "These are they who have come out of the great tribulation; they have washed their robes and made them white in the blood of the Lamb." I said, "I do not know much but I know one thing: my sins have been pardoned and I want to follow my Redeemer wherever He may go before me. No matter how narrow the path, may the Lord help me!"

GOD'S CALLING

God's calling to become a preacher was made real to me at a very young and impressionable age, when I listened to my Father preach on our rented farm. He sat on a stool in front of a table covered with a white cloth. I too made a pulpit in the sandpit and preached to my playmates: "Boys, are you in heaven already?" The boys said, "No!" "Then are you in hell?" I asked. "No, we aren't!" was the response. "Well, then we are still on earth and this word is for us, 'For God so loved the world. . . .'" The wind played like an organ in the treetops.

As a child I also had my first religious experience. One time my father had brought back a big "head" of sugar from the market. (Up until 1940, sugar was sold in big clumps.) When Mother went out to milk the cows, I took a cleaver and broke off some pieces from it and crawled under the bed to eat them. That is how my mother found me. That night I dreamt that I was standing by a ditch and wanted to hide in it because the skies turned fiery red and I heard someone say, "Jesus will come now!" I could not face Him and wanted to hide behind the embankment. But it was as if the ground was sinking under me and I could still see the red sky. Finally I could feel someone tapping me on the shoulder. It was my mother trying to wake me. She was wondering why I was weeping in my sleep. I told her about my dream and we said a prayer. I promised never to steal sugar again and to be a good boy.

Our seminary students Aleksander Kuum, Jaan Puskay, Martin Krüger (who later changed his name to Kuigre), Alfred Tõns, Voldemar Ojasson (later Ojassoo).

This childlike faith lasted until I started school. In a small town like Tapa everyone knew my father held worship services in our home and I, age 12, assisted him by accompanying the hymns on a reed organ and even conducting a small choir, thus earning the nick name "St. George's pup." I, on the other hand, did not want to be called that name and wanted to show that I was just as mischievous as all the other boys. As a result, I stopped praying.

When I finally regained my faith, I wanted to pray and preach again. Dr. George A. Simons, Superintendent of The Methodist Episcopal Church in the Baltics, having heard about my conversion, recommended that I take up studies in the German Methodist preacher's seminary in Frankfurt am Main. I gladly accepted the offer and studied there between 1922 and 1924.

TAPA CONGREGATION

At the dedication service of the Tapa congregation. In the front row, first from the left is Karl Kuum, seated in the middle is Superintendent George A. Simons. Aleksander Kuum is in the back row, second from the left.

I was present at the consecration of the new Methodist church building in Tapa. Sister Nelke, one of the original church members in Tapa, and a good friend of the family, seeing me for the first time since my conversion, clapped her hands together in amazement and shouted, "Aleksander, you look altogether different!" The congregation requested Superintendent Simons to appoint me as their preacher. As there was a shortage of spiritual workers, their request was granted; and so it was that I accepted a position of responsibility as the elder of the Tapa congregation at such an early age and in my hometown nonetheless. Regardless, my memories of my first appointment are the very best indeed.

TARTU CONGREGATION

In 1926, when Brother Johannes Karlson applied to go to study in a seminary in America, I was appointed to continue his work in the Methodist congregation in the city of Tartu, where he had started a church three years earlier. I worked there for 12 years and these were the tensest years of my service. It started with the need for a new church building. The building cost some 45.000 Estonian kroons and we had no money. The story of turning the Zoege von Manteuffel villa in the center of Tartu at 18 Vallikraavi Street into a "Methodist paradise" was a major prayer request and a sheer miracle. A small group of believers soon grew into a 200-member congregation with a large Sunday school, youth club, choir, string orchestra, and brass band. Social work of the congregation was channeled through the Mutual Aid Society, which was involved in serving free lunches during the depression, ran a shelter, and collected secondary raw materials to be sold for recycling for funding their charity work. My social activity in the position as the chairman of the Temperance Movement and chairman of the Sunday School Alliance, director of publishing and editor of the Kristlik Kaitsja (Christian Advocate) magazine, member of Tartu city council and the adoptions court all belong in this same time period. I also contributed to the work of the alliance conferences and committees responsible for organizing prayer weeks, as well as the new church hymnal among others.

Consequently, for social and philanthropic activities I was awarded the order of the Red Cross, IV class, on February 21, 1940, by the State Head of Estonia.

TALLINN CONGREGATION

In 1938, I was appointed to the Tallinn congregation and I felt like an uprooted tree. I found a small congregation in a huge church building at 4A Veerenni Street, with a costly and extensive

Agathe and Aleksander in Tartu in 1928.

renovation in progress. The start of World War II and general mobilization, which took many of the men to Russia along with many other sorrowful events described below, introduced a whole new era to my life as I knew it.

Now, in retrospect, I find myself thinking with amazement that it is over 20 years since I moved to Tallinn and God has allowed many hardships to be turned into blessings. This congregation with its 150 members has grown to be one of the largest congregations in the family of Estonian believers. We have managed to get a congregational building under roof in the historic old city. It has been such a blessing to be able to work together in harmony with Brother Hugo Oengo, 13 deacons, and many young brothers. Holding 7 worship services each week in a roomy church building on Mere Puiestee Street, always full of attendants – this is a living witness to the risen Lord's promise,

"And surely I will be with you always, to the very end of the age" (Matthew 28:20).

The Tallinn Church at 4A Veerenni Street, which was destroyed in the March 9, 1944, bombing raid of the city by the Red Army air force.

It is now nearly dawn, and I have let some 60 years pass by from a bird's-eye view, both the joys and the sorrows. What, I ask myself, in all of this has been closest to my heart? I have loved my work as an elder. Even though my sons have good jobs, I tell them, "I expect you to be my successors – there is no work more beautiful than the work of blessing human souls." Music and songs have been very close to my heart, and to this day I have not set aside the conductor's baton. I have also enjoyed writing and publishing. Every new issue of the magazine, each new book from the printing press was just like a new baby to me, always giving me joy. However, the most precious of all has been the work of evangelizing. To kneel at the foot of the cross with a sinner, to see the joy of salvation in their eyes, makes me feel young again; and it makes all the suffering seem inconsequential. Nothing can be compared to being saved and fighting for another to be saved.

Aleksander Kuum preaching in the church at 3 Mere Puiestee in Tallinn.

YEARS OF SUFFERING

Since I mentioned suffering, let me add a few words about that as well. Until I was 40 I did not know what hardships and suffering were. At times I asked in all seriousness, "Don't you love me, God? Since those you love you discipline (Proverbs 3:12), don't you?" But all was well in my life. I have never been really ill. Everything I undertook went well. Since 1928, I was happily married. My wife, Agathe Rokk, had been born into the family of a parish school master and public figure; and God gave us seven strong and healthy children, five boys and two girls. We loved and we were loved. There was only one problem, why are there no problems?

But then the times of trouble came, and we learned to appreciate another kind of blessing – God's presence amidst hardships. First of all I would like to mention the notorious night of March 9, 1944, when our church building on Veerenni Street was destroyed by the Red Army in an aerial bombing raid of

Tallinn. Along with the church, we lost the parsonage, as well as all of our personal belongings. Everything we had worked for was gone in one night. My first emotion was of a broken man, too old to start afresh. It was difficult to accept that I had lost both my church and my home. As I was standing in front of the smoldering ruins, something rolled out of the pile of smoking ashes and caught my eye. It was the metal baptismal bowl, given to us by the Tartu congregation, which read "Let the little children come to me." And all of a sudden my heart was filled with gladness. "No, you are not impoverished, you have seven children! No, you are not unemployed, even if you do not have a church to preach in."

Aleksander Kuum in Siberia, May 1, 1956.

But the next blow was even harder: our 13-year-old son was killed in an accident. When I carried his lifeless body home from the field, I realized how precious he was. It was the heaviest burden of my life.

Last but not least, there was the third blow. I was sentenced to 25 years in Siberia, which meant I would be separated from my work , home, family, and love.

Nevertheless, it is through these hardships I have learned more than in the good days. Now I know that God loves me too. I have felt it particularly in moments when I have had no other hope left but Him.

Mem'ries of the life behind me –
how I love and fear them though,
years were filled with so much beauty,
all the greyer life seems now.

> But I'd rather choose to suffer
> Than to forfeit Mem'ry Lane
> Which contains much joy and beauty
> happiness and even pain.

God has marked my point of crossing
I've still time to walk this shore,
and when I look back for the last time
oh wonder! The pain will be no more.

Remembering Aleksander Kuum

By Olav Pärnamets, Superintendent Emeritus, The UMC in Estonia

The following account was written by Olav Pärnamets, who had the privilege of working alongside Superintendent Kuum for many years. Aleksander Kuum led the Tallinn Methodist Congregation from 1938 to 1952 and from 1956 to 1970, before passing this baton on to Olav Pärnamets. So too, the position of superintendent, which Aleksander Kuum held from 1962 to 1974 and again from 1978 to 1979 was in turn passed on to Reverend Pärnamets who went on to serve the church in this capacity from 1979 to 2005.

At the Pärnamets' house in 1951. In the front row, first person from the left is young Olav Pärnamets. Second row, from left to right: Agathe Kuum, Johannes Pärnamets, Aleksander Kuum, Meeta Pärnamets.

Aleksander Kuum was one of those very inspirational people. His life and work has meant a great deal to those of us who have had the privilege to know him, to see and to hear him, to have him as mentor and a coworker.

For myself it all began one November evening in 1951 when my parents, who had joined the Tallinn Methodist Congregation, took me, a sickly 14-year-old boy suffering from tuberculosis, along to a prayer meeting. Aleksander Kuum, a true champion of soul-winning evangelists, could turn not only a prayer meeting but any occasion – be it wedding or birthday party – into a revival meeting. "Is there anybody here today who wishes to dedicate his or her life to God?" he asked and with a smile cast a glance across the large audience. For a moment, his gaze fixed on me, and after a short inner struggle, I stood up as an indication of my decision to follow Jesus.

This encounter took place in the Seventh Day Adventist church building on Mere Puiestee, Tallinn. The spacious Methodist church in Tallinn had been destroyed along with many other residential buildings on March 9, 1944, in the Soviet Red Army bombing raid of Tallinn. The second Methodist church building, spared in the bombing of the city, was soon confiscated by the Soviet occupying forces. However, it was God's will that the plans of the Soviet functionaries to do away with The Methodist Church in Estonia would not succeed. The Soviets considered it risky to leave a thriving congregation without a chance to gather for worship services that could be legally and openly regulated. It was a larger headache for the Soviets to deal with so-called "underground churches." However, the plans to annihilate The Methodist Church in Estonia were not discarded. In neighboring Russia, Latvia, and Lithuania, the Methodist work was completely liquidated; and certainly this was the Soviet intention for Estonia as well. I have been asked on many occasions, how it was possible for the Methodist work to survive in Estonia despite the half century of occupation that was so hostile toward religion. I have responded by saying that first, it has been by the great and inexplicable grace of God. Second, I attribute it to the fact that the vast majority of Estonian Methodist clergy remained in Estonia at a time when the Red Army, together with their Moscow-appointed "Kremlin regents," took over Estonia. Soviet forces had already briefly occupied Estonia for two terribly repressive years from 1940 to 1941 at the onset of World War II[33]. As the war drew toward its close, and the Soviet forces were set to return, tens of thousands of Estonians escaped to the West as refugees. The memories of the first Soviet occupation with its mass repressions that took thousands to the GULAG in Siberia or ended innocent lives in summary executions were still fresh in their minds. It is not surprising therefore, that among those running from the Red tidal wave there were also pastors, for the hostile attitude of the atheistic Soviet authorities towards religion and especially Christianity was well known.

Undoubtedly, Aleksander Kuum had a chance to flee to the West along with others; however, he did not use this opportunity. The role of the head of the church was *de facto* placed upon the shoulders of Aleksander Kuum, following the arrest of Superintendent Martin Prikask in 1941, as well as the mobilization of tens of thousands of Estonian men, including Pastor Hugo Oengo, drafted to the Red Army and sent to the work battalions at the Soviet rear.

As is characteristic of totalitarian regimes, decisions made by government officials are executed by the political secret police – in the Soviet Union it was the KGB. Key persons were summoned

---

[33] This reign of terror was interrupted when German forces pushed the Red Army out, and inflicted their own occupation on Estonia from 1941 to 1944. (Translator's note)

to be interrogated in the *carrot and stick style:* those who do not accept the carrot will have to consider tasting the alternative, that is, the stick.

Aleksander Kuum could only guess what was in store for him, when one day prior to 1950, he was summoned to KGB headquarters in Tallinn for an "interview," as interrogations were commonly referred to by the secret police. It turned out that all they needed was the signature of the head of The Methodist Church to a previously drawn-up document stating that the aforementioned signatory agrees of his own free will to the dissolution of The Methodist Church in Estonia. The members of the Methodist congregations were to be divided up among the churches that for the time being the Soviet government had agreed to tolerate as a necessary evil. According to Soviet ideology, belief in God was a serious snag on society's road toward the "bright future" of humankind, that is, communism. Therefore the rule of thumb was: making it as bad as possible for the church is making it better for the Soviets.

But let us return to the moment when Pastor Aleksander Kuum enters the KGB interrogation room thick with tobacco smoke. Our beloved pastor is troubled, but not frightened and not a bit filled with panic. In prayer he trusts his family, his church, and himself into the hands of Him who is greater than our problems. The KGB officer seated at the table, points at a chair and says, "Sit down."

The 50-year-old dignified servant of God with strands of silver in his hair sits, and the interrogator starts with the introductory questions from his "standard repertoire" to establish the identity of Aleksander Kuum, pastor of the Tallinn Methodist Congregation. Obviously the interrogator is not an ordinary functionary, and he realizes quite soon that Aleksander Kuum is not a man willing to sign anything simply out of fear of the notorious secret police. The interrogator comes to the main part of the "interview." Candidly, he reveals the plans of the Communist Party and the Soviet government: "The Estonian Methodist Church as such will be dissolved!" "Dissolved? Why? How?" asks Pastor Kuum in return, knowing full well the answers to his questions. "Why?" repeats the KGB officer, "because your church is spreading harmful ideology, that's why. The leadership of your church includes people such as Martin Prikask, found guilty of anti-Soviet propaganda, and you are in contact with forces in the West hostile to the socialist cause."

"We are no longer in contact with anybody in the West," Kuum parries immediately.

"Do you think that we do not know, what you have personally written in your magazine concerning the situation of churches in the Soviet Union?" With these words the KGB officer hands Kuum a typed document stating that as an authorized representative of The Estonian Methodist Church, the signatory to the document agrees to the liquidation of The EMC in the territory of the Soviet Republic of Estonia. In addition, it was demanded that Pastor Kuum hand over, most likely as a symbol of submission, the keys to the Tallinn Methodist Church (commonly referred to as the Petlemma Congregation) to the respective "authorities."

"No, I will not do that," said Brother Kuum quietly but with confidence. The officer was unpleasantly surprised by the pastor's obstinacy and his tone of voice started to sound more threatening.

"Your refusal does not change anything. Your church is going to be liquidated despite your opposition," he announced, spelling every word out carefully. "We recommend that you choose an option that is safest for you personally. Do not forget that we have the power."

No, Brother Kuum had not forgotten the tragic facts of the mass deportation of tens of thousands of Estonians into the Siberian concentration camps. However, he also had not forgotten that God is in control in every circumstance and it is up to Him to say the last and decisive word.

"Listen, Citizen Aleksander Kuum, come to your senses! The end result is going to be exactly the same, the dissolution of The EMC. I cannot see any difference here worth mentioning."

And suddenly, in such an unusual place and even to Brother Kuum's surprise, the preacher in him was awakened.

"Let me explain my refusal," he said. Ignoring the impatience of the KGB officer, he continued, "Let's say, for example, that you wanted to get rid of me but did not wish to soil your hands, instead you handed me a long piece of rope with a recommendation, 'go and hang yourself.' If I took your advice and killed myself, I would be held responsible before God and men (since I have not given myself my own life, I have no right to end it). But if you would hang me, you would be held responsible before God Almighty and the people. As you can see, the difference is quite remarkable." Evidently this meaningful short sermon gave food for thought, even for an employee of the infamous three-letter organization. God's ways are mysterious indeed. Although, by order of the government, the only remaining Methodist church building in Tallinn was taken away in 1950, shortly after this "interview," the congregation survived, as did most Methodist congregations in Estonia. Once again, as Christians have experienced throughout the centuries, difficult times do not necessarily mean bad times. All things work together for good for those who love God.

The Tallinn Methodist Congregation was left without a building, but God arranged so that the church was able to use the rooms of the Seventh Day Adventist building, situated at No. 3 Mere Puiestee. [I must clarify that, according to Soviet law, all church buildings as well as the furnishings belonged to the state. Therefore the State was at liberty to take away church buildings without compensation or rent them back to the churches and leave the renovations and all financial burdens on the congregation. The Soviet policy meant, for example, that the church had to pay a higher price for electricity than anyone else. As a "bonus," pastors and church organists in the Soviet Union had more taxes deducted from their salaries than other professionals, and so on. The officials therefore, did not even have to ask the Adventists for their consent to this arrangement, a scheme that was applied in other cases as well. There are cases in Estonia where there were some three or more congregations crammed into one church building.]

If God allows something to be taken from us, then He replaces it with something better. So it was that the new building turned out to be in a much more strategic location compared to the location of the Petlemma Church. First, it had a bigger church hall, complete with central heating. Second, it had nearly ideal access for the public. The officials said that the Methodists were allowed to stay there only three months. Obviously they were hoping that they could get rid of the troublesome Methodists altogether. However, God had different plans for us and He allowed us to meet in that building for 50 fruitful years. The membership of the congregation multiplied, and 1957 marked the start of the Methodist work in the Russian language. Finally in the year 2000, ten and a half years after brother Kuum's death, our new church building was completed with the generous aid of our American and Korean sister churches. Under the very roof there live side-by-side the Russian- and Estonian-speaking congregation as well as the Baltic Methodist Theological Seminary.

But let us return to the early 1950's. In addition to the fact that Aleksander Kuum was accused of being too obstinate, disobedient, and unusually bold in the eyes of KGB, they also accused him of the congregation growing too rapidly in the new location. The congregation attracted a sizable group of youth and I had the privilege to belong to the ranks of these young people. Work with children and youth was strictly forbidden by law in the Soviet Union. The KGB, as the faithful watchdog of the state, tried to single out people who dared to disobey the "pharaoh" and who, despite the ban, were doing children's work under the pretext of family gatherings, etc. Among these people were my parents who opened up their home frequently to the young people and sometimes invited also the pastor to encourage and teach the youth. As it turned out later, there was a KGB agent among the youth, who informed his superiors of everything that he could easily pass as anti-Soviet propaganda. If anyone was branded with that title, it meant severe repressions, as he would be declared an "enemy of the people."

In May 27, 1952, well after midnight, several KGB officials were demanding to be let in to the Kuum residence in Tallinn's historic old city. One of Aleksander Kuum's sons, Leev, who at the time of these events was already a university student, remembers a group of five KGB men barging into their two bedroom apartment on Pikk Street, sometime after midnight. (Incidentally, the apartment building where Aleksander Kuum resided with his family of eight, was basically next door to the KGB headquarters.)

The reason for their midnight "visit" was revealed soon enough: they had come to arrest Aleksander Kuum. Remaining calm, he gathered his wife and children around him and trusted them in prayer to the care and protection of the Almighty One. Although it was not at all to the liking of the men who had come to arrest him, they did not dare interrupt this sorrowful, solemn, yet at the same time hopeful moment of prayer.

"Later I quite frequently ran into the agents who arrested my father on the street close to their 'lair.' Their faces had been imprinted in my memory ever since that grim night. When we accidentally met on the street, they made an effort to look aside as if I was a total stranger," reminisces Leev Kuum.

It was not until the next morning that the rest of us found out what had happened at the home of Aleksander Kuum during the night.

That night in May has also etched itself indelibly in my mind, for the very night of Kuum's arrest, KGB functionaries also barged into our family home. We had already settled in for the night and were sleeping peacefully, when we were awakened by loud banging on our front door. My father went to answer the door. It turned out that the men standing in the cover of darkness, sent by the very same infamous organization, had orders to conduct a thorough search of our house. Our family was told to go in one room that we were not allowed to leave. It was evident that these people had refined their skills with a lot of experience at going through other people's possessions. With the exception of one person, they did not speak a word of Estonian. The entire house was gone through with a fine-toothed comb. Even the small green shed in the garden was inspected. Nearly all the books were collected from the rooms. Any piece of literature published prior to the Soviet occupation, was confiscated as suspicious, including the gardening handbooks. At the end of their "graveyard shift," the "comrades" from the KGB finished their task of hauling the stack of books into their "black raven" (as the vehicles were called that were used by the KGB to carry their interrogators, search parties, arresting officers, and deportation agents into the homes of millions across the vast territories covered by the communist totalitarian regime). We were told that all confiscated books would be inspected and those not containing anti-Soviet content would be returned to us later. That, however, remained just a promise. A beautiful leather-bound book was treated with particular suspicion. It had been presented to us by the Tallinn congregation as a housewarming present when Aleksander Kuum blessed our new home. On the front pages it had entries from Aleksander Kuum and other friends who attended the festive occasion, expressing their thoughts and wishes, signed with their names. Our uninvited night visitors tore these pages out, without our permission, and took them along as they left. Nevertheless, the men from headquarters did not think it sufficient, and at dawn an errand-boy arrived to fetch the guest book itself, despite the fact that the rest of the pages were empty.

For several months following his arrest, Pastor Aleksander Kuum was held in one of the many cells in the basement of the KGB headquarters on Pagari Street in Tallinn's old city, just a few steps from his family's apartment. As a rule, the interrogations took place at night with the purpose of wearing the detainee out both physically and mentally, driving the detainee to the breaking point when the person would be willing to sign a confession to any charge of which he or she was accused in. Yet Brother Kuum was not alone and forsaken in the midst of these tribulations. I remember our second pastor in the Tallinn congregation, Hugo Oengo, reminding us of the story of the apostle Peter's imprisonment in the Book of Acts: *So Peter was kept in prison, but the church was earnestly praying to God for him* (Acts 12:5). Many Christians in the Tallinn congregation and across Estonia were praying for Aleksander Kuum. And he did not give in. In a few months, in the hall of the Supreme Court, a typical Soviet puppet court hearing was acted out in Tallinn, where the verdict was known long before the session. I (aged 15) was summoned to the hearing as a witness, since I also had been interrogated for hours in the KGB headquarters. My interrogator was a KGB officer with the rank of captain; and as my Russian was not good enough at the time, the interrogation was conducted with the help of a translator. At the court hearing I discovered that my interrogator had included statements in the protocol I had never said. When I shouted out in the courtroom, addressing the judge in shock and resentment, "Bring out the men who have made up such claims!" my testimony was cut short and I was removed from the stand as a witness.

"Be seated!" ordered the judge.

Prior to my testimony, the public prosecutor, who delivered his speech entirely in Russian, spoke passionately, flashing his fiery eyes and actively gesticulating all the while. I, however, could understand almost nothing. Prior to announcing the verdict, the so-called last word was given to the accused. For me it was somewhat strange to see my pastor having buzz cut hair, a "hairdo" that was given to all the prisoners.

I remember the words of Aleksander Kuum, "In deciding upon the verdict, I ask the court to consider my large family who are in the need of my care and support."

The panel of judges disappeared behind closed doors only to resume their seats in their tall chairs in no time at all. The verdict was read out loud, leaving aside all the mumble-jumble of the usual jargon, the verdict itself was quite standard for the Stalinist period. "Twenty-five years in the forced labor camp (the GULAG) with an additional five years of exile in Siberia without the right to repatriate, with full confiscation of all personal property."

The guards, armed with automatic weapons were ordered to take the prisoner away and they immediately gave the order to the convicted prisoner. I followed the line of men accompanying Brother Kuum to the corridor of the courthouse and noticed Aleksander Kuum's wife, Agathe, and his children standing there. Brother Kuum reached out his hands to touch the cheek of his wife and wipe away the tears streaming down her face. Although the guard was quick to wave his gun to prevent contact, this time he was not fast enough. Shortly after these events, the trip to Siberia began for Aleksander Kuum.

Journey to Siberia

The journey to Siberia was long and hard. The destination was the oblast of Irkutsk, which has a territory larger than the state of Texas. The area is situated in the southeastern part of the Central Siberian Plateau. The initial place of his incarceration was the village of Sosnovka in the Tchuna district, situated on the Tchuna River. Later he was detained in the village of Novotchunka in the same area. What he felt and thought as the gates of the Stalinist forced labor camp were shut behind him can only be imagined. He had been taken thousands of kilometers from his country, family, and church. His thoughts on that day are known to God, yet we can get a glimpse of what he was going through in the songs and poetry he wrote during the days and nights spent in the camp.

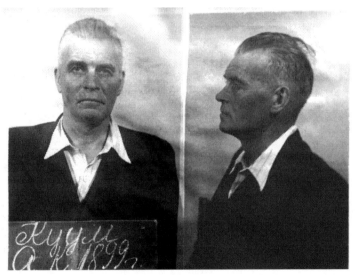

The photograph of Aleksander Kuum, taken following his arrest in May 27, 1952.

Four years later, after having returned to Estonia, he told us, "As soon as I arrived in the camp, I was gradually overcome by the feeling that I am not intended to stay here. As soon as the spring comes, I will escape." Putting such plans into action was, to put it mildly, completely unrealistic. The camp was surrounded by several high barbed wire fences, armed guards were stationed all around in watchtowers. It seemed that even the mosquitoes were unable to fly through the fence without being spotted. Yet, one spring morning, prisoner Aleksander Kuum noticed that the prison gates were standing open as something was being transported into the camp in trucks. Kuum started moving slowly toward the gates, keeping constant watch from the corner of his eye on the nearest watchtowers. Soon he had passed the line that marked where you could be shot without warning. Adrenaline was running high as the Methodist pastor walked, just like the apostle Peter, out of the prison gates. Siberian virgin forest started very close to the camp, "if I can only make it into the forest before the guards notice me and send out a shower of bullets!" thought Kuum. And, low and behold, he made it! Brother Kuum himself attributed the distractedness of the prison guards to a rare visitor in the camp, a woman. It is not known what punish-ment befell the guards, but as soon as it was discovered that there was a prisoner missing, a search was organized. However, one of the locals spotted a man in prisoner's clothes not far from the camp. Kuum was captured, beaten, and yelled at. After having been tied up, he was thrown in the back of a truck and taken back to the camp, where he spent the next six months in solitary confinement. This seemingly depressing period of anguish turned out to be very prol ific in terms of songwriting and poetry. All alone with his God, he turned to Him in prayer: "If you have work for me, I will go out to your harvest, If you need a sacrifice, I will lay myself down on the altar."

It is here in solitary that he wrote most of his Siberian poems, many of which he also set to music. One of his poems was inspired by the words carved into the posts of his cot: "Всё пройдёт" (Everything shall pass).

All things shall pass, bear it well and believe –
even toil and pain serve a purpose . . ..
Everything shall pass, be patient and trust,
That after the rain there'll be a rainbow in the sky...

(He also composed a melody to this poem and later taught the song to our church choir, conducting it personally.)

Brother Kuum did get to see his rainbow. Fortunately for so many political prisoners, Stalin died in 1953 after having managed to kill and torture so many people in his reign, even exceeding Hitler, the other super killer in the history of mankind. Following a power struggle in the Kremlin, Nikita Khrushchev's faction prevailed. Some three years after Stalin's death, he dared to express a few critical comments on his predecessor and former master to appear more democratic in the eyes of the West. In trying to ease the fate of the surviving victims of repressions, the Siberian prison camps were visited by special commissioners from Moscow. Everyone's dossier was read and investigated, prisoners were summoned one by one, and questions were asked. Soon it was Brother Kuum's turn. One of the commissioners, paging through the thick dossier compiled by the KGB, a rich register of "sins," said, "But it says here that you have escaped the prison. Why?"

"I wanted to go home," was the reply. "But this is not possible, there are hundreds, thousands of kilometers of forest and Siberian wilderness; you would not have made it!" the official replied confidently.

The last letter of Aleksander Kuum, written from Siberia.

"Try to put yourself in my shoes," said Brother Kuum, "a man over 50 years of age given the sentence of 25+5 years! Here, far away in Siberia I felt as if I was cast overboard in the middle of the Pacific Ocean. In this situation, a man can choose one of two options: either lose all hope and sink to the bottom, or keep trying to swim and believe in miracles. I tried to swim."

"What will you engage yourself in upon your release?"

"My calling is to preach the joyous gospel of Christ," answered Aleksander Kuum.

This response was not the most pleasing one to the ears of the commissioner, but the outcome of the hearing was positive.

Before his release, Brother Kuum taught the Estonian prisoners in the camp another song: "Let us get going, men, let us start walking toward home. . . ." For Aleksander Kuum, after a period of rain and storm, there was sunshine and a rainbow across the sky.

The following letter is the very last one Aleksander Kuum wrote during his imprisonment and is addressed to Riina Ugand (married name Krupp), whom he called his daughter in faith. It reads as follows:

Siberia, June 20, 1956

Dear Riina,
This is the shortest letter I have written to you. I have just returned from the village where I stood before an important commission which decided to release me from prison. If all goes well, I hope to get my passport tomorrow and maybe as soon as the day after tomorrow be on my way home. I intend to stop over in Moscow for a day and arrive on July 1st or 2nd in Tallinn. Thank you once again for all your love and I'm counting on our joyous meeting back in Tallinn soon.

Yours,

A. Kuum

P.S. Greet your mother and young friends from me!

July 1, 1956, was a memorable day when on a Sunday evening Aleksander Kuum, smiling radiantly, stepped through the door of the church on Mere Puiestee in Tallinn. Everyone gathered for the service stood up and Brother Kuum kneeled in his usual place by the altar. Many had tears of joy and thanksgiving in their eyes.

Aleksander Kuum has often called his experience in Siberia "his university." We never saw any sign of bitterness toward Russians in his behavior. He never blamed the Russians for what had happened; to the contrary, he said that Russians themselves have been the greatest victims of this godless regime. Soon after Aleksander Kuum's return, the Russian work was officially started in the Tallinn congregation of The Methodist Church, which to this day has grown into a vital congregation.

In 1962, Aleksander Kuum was elected Superintendent.

In 1970, I was appointed by Aleksander Kuum to serve in Tallinn Methodist Congregation. Following my appointment, there was a required visit to be paid to the Commissioner of Religious Affairs. This official was essentially an arm of the government to control the activities of the churches and congregations. Brother Kuum, a bit over 70, but very fit, dignified, and possessing a marvelous sense of humor, accompanied me.

"How is the health of the superintendent?" asked the Commissioner, to start the conversation.

"Praise the Lord, considering my age, I have excellent health," replied Kuum with a wide smile. He proceeded to tread on a sensitive issues with the Soviet official, "Prior to having been sent to Siberia, I had rheumatism in my joints; however, while in Siberia, I was rid of my ailments. It must be due to the good climate, I figure." Saying this he felt his shoulder and said, "Lately though, it has started to act up again." Laughing, he added, "Maybe it is telling me I might be sent back again."

The Commissioner and his deputy put on a sour smile. Kuum did not harbor bitter feelings, and the people responsible for his tribulations on the opposite side knew that.

Aleksander Kuum, while not perfect, was nonetheless a man after God's own heart. In him there burned a sacred passion to win people for the Lord. He was always troubled if he noticed that a similar active passion was not present in the hearts of his co-workers. An altar call was always to be given at the end of a service. If not, using the words of Aleksander Kuum himself, the pastor had "failed to pull in the fishing nets to check whether a fish or two had been caught." Time and time again, I have heard him say, "My greatest joy is to kneel with a sinner, under the cross of Jesus, where he or she can leave an old life in order to receive a new one."

Aleksander Kuum in his Tallinn home on Apteegi Street in February 1957.

In his 80's, Aleksander Kuum began to suffer from memory loss. However, he never forgot his own golden rule, which he had been true to all his life: to be involved in the work and to remain in Christian fellowship. He was always present, every Sunday, for fellowship with his congregation or, when on vacation far from a Methodist church, he would visit his neighbors for Christian fellowship. He said that after a time of fellowship even God's creation appears much more beautiful.

Later in life when he was not involved in the ministry of the church, he was still connected through his calling, which compelled him to attend every church conference and meeting that I was leading at the time. On one occasion, when it was time to speak, I noticed our patriarch giving me the sign asking for permission to speak to the audience. "Yes, please, you may speak," I said. "If The Methodist Church does not evangelize," said Brother Kuum, getting up slowly, "then it has no right to exist. Please remember this important point." The truth is that by this point, in addition to memory loss, Aleksander Kuum was also suffering from considerable loss of hearing, and he was never comfortable using a hearing aid. As a result, he was unable to keep up with the current topic of discussion. Having given his message, he sat down. The conference continued. Approximately twenty minutes later, I noticed his hand going up again. I looked at him and allowed him to speak again. "If The Methodist Church does not evangelize and win souls over for Jesus, then it has no right to exist," he repeated. Wrapped up in this statement is his deep conviction, his legacy that he wanted to pass on to us before his life came to an end. This was something so brightly implanted in his mind that it could not be eradicated by loss of hearing or memory.

Lord have mercy on us! Help us to be true Methodists!

The Lord raised his loyal servant to glory on February 12, 1989. A great crowd sent him off on his last journey in St. Olav's

Church in Tallinn. His earthly remains are buried under the pine trees in Tallinn's Rahumäe Cemetery.

I am utterly grateful to God for Aleksander Kuum, who invited me to follow Jesus and through whom I, as well as many others, were called to serve the Lord.

Remember your leaders, who spoke the word of God to you. Consider the outcome of their way of life and imitate their faith.

Hebrews 13:7

AN INTERNATIONAL TRIBUTE

When The Methodist Church in Estonia celebrated her 75th anniversary, Aleksander Kuum was awarded with a diploma by the Upper Room, signed by the General Secretary of The UMC Board of Discipleship, Ezra Earl Jones, from Nashville, Tennessee. The diploma was handed to him in Tallinn, on September 13, 1982, by the American representatives. My wife and I were present at the festive occasion, along with many other Estonian Methodist workers, friends, guests, and of course Aleksander Kuum's family. This award was an international recognition for his outstanding work and leadership in the body of Christ. On the occasion, Brother Kuum was characterized as follows:

Follower of Jesus Christ, dedicated Christian and a man of God, whose life has been an excellent example of the quality of life and strength that a true believer should possess.

Evangelist, who under any circumstance preaches the gospel, calling upon the people to give their lives to Christ.

Preacher, whose spirit-filled message conveys the teaching of Christ and is an inspiration to others.

Patriarch of The Methodist Church, whose personal sacrifice and spirituality has helped the church in following the Great Master, Jesus Christ.

Keeper of the Faith, whose clear vision and utter dedication has been an undying spark and ignited many a heart to burn with the flame of faith.

It is difficult to find more nobler and befitting words to describe our beloved brother and superintendent Aleksander Kuum.

Concluding Remarks

I am thrilled to present this book as we celebrate the 100th jubilee of The UMC in Estonia in June of 2007.

For myself, compiling this book about Estonian heroes of the faith was a truly interesting excursion into the past. Studying the biographical materials of Martin Prikask, Jaan Jaagupsoo, Peeter Häng, Vassili Prii, Hugo Oengo, and Aleksander Kuum gave me a new and intimate perspective into the lives of these heroes of the cross, who in the circumstances of the totalitarian state had to pay the highest price for their faith. The lives and suffering of such men are an inseparable and intrinsic part of our Estonian history as well as our rich global Methodist heritage.

I am pleased if I have succeeded in filling in a few blanks in the story of The Methodist Church in Estonia. I hope this book will be a blessing to all its readers and an encouragement to believers across the world.

I extend heartfelt thanks to the sponsors of this project: the Estonian Council of Churches and Alison & Robert F. Hogan, Jr, from the USA, who covered the publishing as well as translation costs of the English edition of this book. I am grateful to Superintendent Emeritus Olav Pärnamets for submitting an additional article "Remembering Aleksander Kuum" and to the Director of World Methodist Evangelism, Dr. H. Eddie Fox, for kindly recommending this book to the international audience. I thank my wonderful translator Kai-Ines Nelson and her husband

Mark P. Nelson, a lecturer at our Baltic Methodist Theological Seminary, who contributed the Estonian history sections to provide background information for the benefit of our English readers. I am grateful to Tarmo Lilleoja for publishing advice and the necessary maps, and to our proofreader Norma Bates of the Bates Corporation.

I extend thanks to those people who kindly shared their photographs to be used in this book. These people include: Eino Pärnamets, Ralf-Engelhard Uusmäe, Arvi Lindmäe, Helgi-Anne Trumm, Mart Abro, Helgi Eenmaa, Riina Krupp, Liis Oengo, Mildrid-Leida Ojassoo, Salme Klaas, Rutt Wahlström, Laas Helde, Leevi Hark, and Helmet Saupõld. I also thank Saaremaa Museum for allowing me to use a couple of photographs from their collection.

But the biggest praise belongs to our Lord, who inspired me to collect the materials on the heroes of faith of The UMC in Estonia and put together this mosaic of collective memory.

Toomas Pajusoo,
The author

BIBLIOGRAPHY

Superintendent and Martyr Martin Prikask

Ajalooarhiiv, f 1275, n 1, s 473. EELK Halliste kogudus. Meetrikaraamat (1877), p. 16.

Ajalooarhiiv, f 3150, n 1, s 707. EELK Tartu Peetri kogudus. Personaalraamat. P (I pihtkond). XXVIa köide (1870–1909), p. 49.

Eesti Entsüklopeedia, 6 (1992). Mulgimaa. Tallinn: Kirjastus "Valgus", p. 442.

Eesti Metodisti Kiriku teatmik (1995). Kirikuvalitsuse väljaanne, p. 41.

EMK superintendendid (1997). *Koduteel*, nr 7 (32), p.12.

Eestimaa Piiskopliku Methodisti Koguduse Põhjuskiri 1920. Kuressaare. Trükitud T. Liiw'i trükikojas.

Eesti Riigiarhiivi Filiaal (1873), f 4-K, n 2, s 3860. PRIIKASK, Peeter Pritsu p. Pärnumaa. PRIIKASK, Salme Peetri t. 1916 Pärnumaa. PRIIKASK, Tiina Jüri t. 1883 Pärnumaa.

Eesti Riigiarhiivi Filiaal (1873), f 8SM, n 1, s 11057. PRIIKASK, Peeter Prits. Pärnumaa.

Fomitsev, Leeni (2006). A telephone interview with a grandchild of Peeter Priikask, on March 31.

Henno, Tiit 1997. Emakogudus Kuressaare. Koduteel, nr 7(32), november, p. 4.

Kiriku peakoosolek (1940). Kristlik Kaitsja, nr 4, pp. 58–59.

Klaos, Salme (1924). Metodisti kogudused Eestis, nende tekkimine ja arenemine. Diss. Tart. 272195.

Kodumaa teateid (1932). *Kristlik Kaitsja*, nr 10, p.152.

Kodumaa teateid (1935). *Kristlik Kaitsja*, nr 4, p. 63.

Kodumaa teateid(1937). *Kristlik Kaitsja*, nr 11, p. 156.

Kuressaare koguduse teateid (1935). *Koduteel*, nr 8, p.40.

Lindmäe, Arvi (1994). *Mis on v. Prikaski täpne surmaaeg?* Private letter, 10. 04. 1994.

Lindmäe, Arvi (2006). Private letter, February, 28.

Luik, Tiiu (1998). Paistu kihelkond. Meie kodulugu, p. 46.

Martin ja Liisi Prikask'ide hõbepulm (1931). *Meie Maa*, nr. 57, 28. mail, p. 1.

Martin Prikask'i kahekordne juubel (1937). *Meie Maa*, nr 158 (2472), 19. novembril, p. 3.

M. Prikask haige (1935). *Meie Maa*, nr 45 (2058), 17. aprillil, p.1.

Metodist-Episkopal-Kyrkans i Finland Årsbok för 1913. Jämte protokoll öfver Årskonferensen i Åbo den 31 Juli–3 Augusti 1913, Borgå 1913. Borgå Boktryckeri.

Metodist-Episkopal-Kyrkans i Finland Årsbok för 1914. Jämte protokoll öfver Årskonferensen i Helsingfors den 27–30 Augusti 1914, Borgå 1914. Borgå Boktryckeri.

Metodist-Episkopal-Kyrkans i Finland Årsbok 1915. Gamlakarleby Metodistkapell.

Metodist-Episkopal-Kyrkans i Finland Årsbok 1916. Utgifven enligt konferensens beslut af Karl Hurtig. Borgå 1916, Borgå Boktryckeri.

Mõnesugust (1922). *Kristlik Kaitsja*, nr 1, p.25.

Mõnesugust (1923). *Kristlik Kaitsja*, nr 7, p. 111.

Nigol, August (1918). Eesti asundused ja asupaigad Wenemaal. Eesti Kirjastuse-Ühisuse „Postimehe" trükk – Tartus.

Oengo, Hugo (1977). Martin Prikaski 100. sünnipäeval 1877–1942, *Killukesi eluloost*, pp. 1–4.

Pajusoo, Toomas (2002). Usumärter Martin Prikask, *Koduteel*, nr 62, pp. 10–12.

Palumäe, Elmar (1974). Martin Prikask, *Elusõnu mitmest suust*, III.

Piir, Enno (1991). Halliste kihelkond: inimkaotused ja repressioonid alates 21. juunist 1940: kihelkondades asuvate valdade piirid, elanikud, seltsid, tööstus, põllumajandus ja olme 1940. aastaks/ "Memento" Viljandi osakond, p. 58.

Prikask, Martin (1924). A letter to S. Klaos, in Kuressaare, October, 9. UMC in Estonia archives.

Prikask, Martin (1929). J. Laar †, *Kristlik Kaitsja*, nr 7, p. 111.

Prikask, Martin (1933). Muudatus "Kristlik Kaitsja" väljaandmises, *Kristlik Kaitsja*, nr 4, p. 61.

Prikask, Martin (1933). Eesti Metodisti Kiriku arenemine ja aastakonverentsid, *Kristlik Kaitsja*, nr 8/9, pp. 120–123.

Prikask, Martin (1935). A letter to the Minister of Defence, p. 1.

Prikask, Martin (1940). Eesti Piiskopliku Metodistikiriku koguduste nimekiri, p. 1.

Rajamaa, Tapani (2006). Personal letter, May 4, 2006, p.1.

Russian Methodists Honor Their First Pioneer (1924). *Methodism in Russia, Latvia, Lithuania and Estonia. A Quarterly Bulletin Published at Riga, Latvia.* April, May, June , lk 7.

Streiff, Patrick Ph. (2003). Methodism in Europe: 19th and 20th century. Baltic Methodist Theological Seminary. pp. 142-145; 183-189

Tamm, Priit (1998). Eesti Metodisti Kirik 1940–1980: Vaatlusi olulisematele arengut mõjutanud protsessidele ja probleemidele. Tartu Ülikooli Usuteaduskond, Ajaloolise usuteaduse ja ladina keele õppetool. Bachelor's Dissertation, Supervisor mag. Riho Altnurme.

Toimetaja aken (1940). Kristlik Kaitsja, nr 6/7, p. 91.

Tombo, Ferdinand (1924). A letter to S. Klaos. Information concerning the Tallinn Methodist Episcopal Church.

Uus Kristlik Kaitsja (1928). *Uus Kristlik Kaitsja,* nr 1, p. 97.

Õispuu, Leo (2001). Küüditamine Eestist Venemaale. Juuniküüditamine 1941 & küüditamised 1940–1953. Tallinn: Eesti Represseeritute Registri Büroo. Raamat 6, p. 574.

Õpetaja M. Prikask'i 50. aasta juubel (1927). *Kristlik Kaitsja,* nr 12, p. 188.

What God Hath Wrought (1924). *Methodism in Russia,Latvia, Lithuania and Estonia. A Quarterly Bulletin Published at Riga, Latvia.* April, May, June , p. 12.

Zwiebelberg, Werner (1942). Halliste kiriku ja kihelkonna ajalugu. Pärnu.

Remembering Martin Prikask

Truu, Johannes (1976). Mida mäletan vend Prikase elust ja tööst? Katkend käsikirjast.

Truu, Johannes (2002). Mälestusi Martin Prikasest, Koduteel, nr 62, p. 13.

First Martyr for the Faith Jaan Jaagupsoo

Balti ja Slaavi aastakonverentsil Riias (1932). *Kristlik Kaitsja,* nr 8/9, p. 133.

Balti ja Slaavi aastakonverents Tallinnas (1933). *Kristlik Kaitsja,* nr 10, p. 141.

Balti ja Slaavi aastakonverentsi määrustik (1929). *Kristlik Kaitsja,* nr 10, p. 156.

Balti ja Slaavi Misjoni poolaastakonverentsi võhik jutlustajate määrustik (1927). *Kristlik Kaitsja,* nr 4, p. 57.

Jakobson, Jaan (1933). Elamusi tööpõldude vahetusel. Kristlik Kaitsja, nr 12, p.182.

Jakobson, Jaan (1933). Mälestusi isa Kuumast. Kristlik Kaitsja, nr 3, p. 40.

Kalm, Salme (2006). A private letter, March 3, 2006.

Kalm, Salme (2006). A Telephone interview from March 3.

Kiriku peakoosolek (1940). *Kristlik Kaitsja*, nr 4, p.59.

Kodumaalt (1930). *Kristlik Kaitsja*, nr 4, p.63.

Kodumaa teateid (1931). *Kristlik Kaitsja*, nr 11, p. 167.

Kodumaa teateid (1933). *Kristlik Kaitsja*, nr 11, p. 168.

Kodumaa teateid (1934). *Kristlik Kaitsja*, nr 11, p.167.

Kodumaa teateid (1935). *Kristlik Kaitsja*, nr 5, p. 79.

Kodumaa teateid (1936). *Kristlik Kaitsja*, nr 3, p. 47.

Kodumaa teateid (1936). *Kristlik Kaitsja*, nr 7/8, p. 111.

Kodumaa teateid (1936). *Kristlik Kaitsja*, nr 9, p. 127.

Kodumaa teateid (1938). *Kristlik Kaitsja*, nr 4, p. 62.

Kodumaa teateid (1939). *Kristlik Kaitsja*, nr 5, p. 79.

Kodumaa teateid (1939). *Kristlik Kaitsja*, nr 11, p. 144.

Laar, Mart ja Tross, Jaan (1996). Punane terror. Välis-Eesti & EMP, Stockholm, p. 188.

Metodisti koguduse juubel (1938). *Lääne Elu*, 11. märts.

Perekonna teateid (1934). *Kristlik Kaitsja*, nr 8/9, p. 135.

Perekonna teateid (1934). *Kristlik Kaitsja*, nr 11, p. 167.

Perekonna teateid (1935). *Kristlik Kaitsja*, nr 4, p. 63.

Perekonna teateid (1936). *Kristlik Kaitsja*, nr 11, p. 160.

Perekonna teateid (1939). *Kristlik Kaitsja*, nr 11, p. 144.

Puskay, Jaan (1933). *Mõnda üksikkoguduste ajaloost, Kristlik Kaitsja*, nr 8/9, p. 132.

Rebane, Lea (2006). A telephone interview from February 16.

Rebane, Lea (2006). An interview from May, 8.

Ritsbek, Heigo (1993). *Estonian Methodism during the first year under the plague of the Red Commissars, Methodist History, 31:4, July*, p. 252.

Toimetaja aken (1934). *Kristlik Kaitsja*, nr 2, p. 28.

Toimetaja aken (1934). *Kristlik Kaitsja*, nr 6, p. 90.

Viivik, Allar (2004). *Paadipõgenikud kogesid tormi, nälga ja hirmu, SL Õhtuleht*, laupäev, 25. september.

Wahlström, Rutt (2006). A telephone conversation from March, 20.

Wahlström, Rutt (2006). Private letter, dated March, 29.

Martyr for the Faith Peeter Häng

Balti ja Slaavi aastakonverents (1932). *Kristlik Kaitsja*, nr 8/9, p. 133.

Eesti Riigiarhiiv, f 1108, n 15, s 70. Õpetaja Lydia Dsiss'i, mehe järele Häng, teenistuskiri.

Eesti Riigiarhiiv, f 1108, n 15, s 71. Õpetaja Peeter Häng'i teenistuskiri.

Eesti Riigiarhiiv, f 1108, n 15, s 219. Õpetaja August Mälk'i teenistuskiri.

Helde, Laas (1975). *Metodismi tulekust Torku, Studia Methodistica teoloogilisi materjale iseõppijaile* I. Tallinn: Kirikuvalitsuse väljaanne.

Helde, Laas (2006). An interview from March, 15.

Häng, Leevi (2006). Private letter, dated February 28.

Häng, Leevi (2006). A telephone interview from March 1.

Häng, Peeter (1933). *Isiklikke mälestusi Karl Kuumast, Kristlik Kaitsja* nr 3, p. 38.

Kiriku peakoosolek (1940). *Kristlik Kaitsja*, nr 4, p. 59.

Kodumaa teateid (1931). *Kristlik Kaitsja*, nr 11, p. 167.

Kodumaa teateid (1932). *Kristlik Kaitsja*, nr 8/9, p. 136.

Kodumaa teateid (1939). *Kristlik Kaitsja*, nr 8/9, p. 111.

Kodumaa teateid (1940). *Kristlik Kaitsja* nr 1, p. 15.

Lindmäe, Arvi (2006). Private letter, dated February 28.

Ojassoo, Valdo (1937). *Muljeid Saaremaa reisilt, Kristlik Kaitsja* nr 1, p. 11.

Saare Maa-arhiiv (1989), f 347, n 3, s 462. Kingissepa Rajooni Rahvasaadikute Nõukogu Täitevkomitee. Toimik 238. Häng, Leevi Peetri p. avaldus massirepressiooni läbi tekitatud materiaalse kahju hüvitamiseks.

Toimetaja aken (1934). *Kristlik Kaitsja* nr 2, p.28.

Toimetaja aken (1937). *Kristlik Kaitsja* nr 10, p. 141.

Välja, Inna (1997). Laas Helde mälestused. An interview from December 12.

Martyr for the Faith Vassili Prii

Aastakonverents (1929). *Kristlik Kaitsja*, nr 10, p.143.

Balti ja Slaavi aastakonverentsi määrustik (1929). *Kristlik Kaitsja*, nr 10, p. 156.

Balti ja Slaavi aastakonverents (1931). *Kristlik Kaitsja*, nr 10, p. 149.

Balti ja Slaavi aastakonverents (1932). *Kristlik Kaitsja*, nr 8/9, p. 133.

Balti ja Slaavi aastakonverents Tallinnas (1933). *Kristlik Kaitsja*, nr 10, p. 142.

Balti ja Slaavi aastakonverents (1939). *Kristlik Kaitsja*, nr 8/9, p. 103.

Baltija Slaavi Misjoni poolaastakonverentsi võhikjutlustajate määrustik (1927). *Kristlik Kaitsja*, nr 4, p. 57.

Eesti Metodisti Kiriku teatmik (1995). Kirikuvalitsuse väljaanne, p. 42–43.

Kiriku erakorraline aastakonverents Tallinnas (1935). *Kristlik Kaitsja*, nr 10, p. 149.

Kiriku peakoosolek (1940). *Kristlik Kaitsja*, nr 4, p. 59.

Kodumaalt (1930). *Kristlik Kaitsja*, nr 12, p. 183.

Kodumaa teateid (1933). *Kristlik Kaitsja*, nr 11, p. 168.

Kodumaa teateid (1935). *Kristlik Kaitsja*, nr 10, p. 150.

Kodumaa teateid (1936). *Kristlik Kaitsja*, nr 9, p. 127–128.

Lindmäe, Arvi (2006). Erakiri.

Lühike ülevaade Paide koguduse palvela muretsemisest (1937). *Kristlik Kaitsja*, nr 2, p. 27

Ojassoo, Valdo (1937). *Muljeid Saaremaa reisilt, Kristlik Kaitsja* nr 1, p. 11.

Perekonnateateid (1935). *Kristlik Kaitsja*, nr 11, p. 164.

Prii, Vassili (1932). *Jumala riigi tööst Viljandis, Kristlik Kaitsja*, nr 6, p. 91.

Prii, Vassili (1933). *Mõtteid venna K. Kuuma surma puhul, Kristlik Kaitsja* nr 3, p. 42.

Prii, Vassili (1935). *Minu jõulutunnistus, Kristlik Kaitsja*, nr 12, p. 169.

Prii, Vassili (1935). *Tartu Ühisabi 5 aastane, Kristlik Kaitsja,* nr 2, p. 27.

Prikask, Martin (1930). *Lühikene reisi ülevaade, Kristlik Kaitsja*, nr 6, p. 90.

Puskay, Jaan (1933). "Mõnda üksikkoguduste ajaloost", *Kristlik Kaitsja*, nr 8/9, p. 131.

Saare Maa-arhiiv (1990), f 347, n 3, s 417. Saare Maavalitsus. Toimik 140. Prii, Marta Sandri t. avaldus massirepressiooni läbi tekitatud materiaalse kahju hüvitamiseks.

Teateid kodumaalt (1932). *Kristlik Kaitsja*, nr 3, p. 48.

Teateid kodumaalt (1932). *Kristlik Kaitsja*, nr 4, p. 64.

Teateid kodumaalt (1933). *Kristlik Kaitsja*, nr 1, p. 16.

Toimetaja aken (1934). *Kristlik Kaitsja*, nr 5, p. 75.

Uue kiriku õnnistamine Pöidel (1932). *Kristlik Kaitsja*, nr 6, pp. 93–94.

Vene misjoni konverentsi ja Baltimaade misjoni määruste leht (1923). *Kristlik Kaitsja*, nr 9, p. 140.

Ärkamine Abruka saarel (1929). *Kristlik Kaitsja*, nr 4, p. 62.

Superintendent Hugo Oengo

Eenma, Helgi (1986). *Mälestused oma isast.* Käsikiri.

Eenma, Helgi (2006). Oral statement, February 27, 2006.

Eesti Metodisti Kirik 1975–1976 (1977). *Studia Methodistica teoloogilisi materjale iseõppijale* II, Kirikuvalitsuse väljaanne, Tallinn.

Elliott, Mark (1991). *Methodism in the Soviet Union Since World War II, The Asbury Theological Journal*, Vol. 46 No. 1. Spring.

Hannele (1977). *Lähettiläs Eestistä, Rauhan Sanomia*, Joulukuu, 84. vuosikerta N:o 13–14, p. 14.

Kiriku erakorraline aastakonverents Tallinnas (1935). *Kristlik Kaitsja*, nr 10, p. 148.

Klementi, J., Mäker, E. (1968). *Meie juubilare. Hugo Oengo 60-aastane, TMK Laualeht*, nr 2.

Kodumaa teateid (1934. *Kristlik Kaitsja*, nr 8/9, p. 134.

Kodumaa teateid (1934. *Kristlik Kaitsja*, nr 11, p. 166.

Kodumaa teateid (1935. *Kristlik Kaitsja*, nr 2, p. 31.

Oengo, Hugo (1960. *Hugo Gustavi pg. Õngo-Oengo elulugu*. Eesti Metodisti kiriku arhiiv.

Oengo, Hugo (1975. *Eluloo kirjeldus*. Manuscript. Dated December 11, 1975 in Tallinn.

Oengo, Hugo (1976. Анкета – Энго-Оэнго Хуго Густовович. Käsikiri. Tallinn, 19. veebruar.

Perekonna teateid (1933. *Kristlik Kaitsja*, nr 6, p. 96.

Pikner, M. (1985). *Kogudusemaja – 25. Tee*, Tallinna Metodisti Kirik.

Tallinnan kirje (1976). *Rauhan Sanomia*, Toukokuu, 83. vuosikerta N:o 6, p. 4.

Tapani (1977). *Vuosikonferenssi Vesivehmaalla 3.–7.8. "Elävä seurakunta toteutumassa", Rauhan Sanomia*, Heinäkuu, 84. vuosikerta N:o 8, p. 6.

Superintendent Aleksander Kuum

Balti ja Slaavi Misjonikonverentsi määrused (1924). Kristlik

Kaitsja, nr 10, p. 155.

Kava (1924). *Piiskopliku Methodisti kiriku sisseõnnistamisel Tapal, Eestis.* Pühapäeval, 17. augustil.

Kleis, R. (1932). *Eesti avalikud tegelased.* Eluloolisi andmeid. Eesti Kirjanduse Selts Tartus, p. 129.

Remembering Aleksander Kuum

Õispuu, Leo (1998). Political arrests in Estonia Under Soviet Occupation. Volume 2. Tallinn, p. 203.

MAPS

Estonia and the Baltic Sea Region.

Registered Congregations of the Methodist Episcopal Church
in Estonia, January 1, 1940.

Borders shown are the internationally recognized borders of the Republic of Estonia from
February 2, 1920 - August 6, 1940 as defined by the Tartu Peace Treaty.

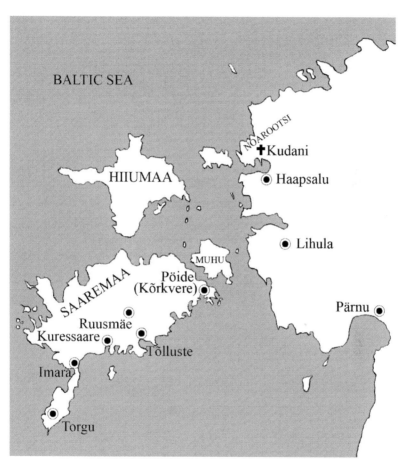

Western Estonia and the Islands, the Birthplace of Estonian Methodism.
✝ indicates the place of Jaan Jaagupsoo's execution.

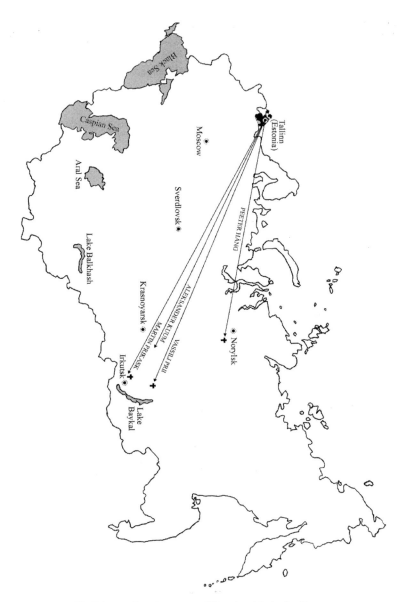

The Siberian Imprisonments of Estonian Methodist Pastors.

Made in the USA
Columbia, SC
06 September 2023

22499527R00093